MY PARISH IS REVOLTING

MY PARISH IS REVOLTING

Norman Ellis

PaperJacks

A division of General Publishing Co. Limited
Don Mills, Ontario

First published by PaperJacks
A division of
General Publishing Company Limited,
Don Mills, Ontario

ISBN 0-7737-7080-1
Printed and bound in Canada
1 2 3 4 5 WO 78 77 76 75 74

CONTENTS

Author's Note   *vii*

Prologue   1

Chapter I. The Place, the People   5

Chapter II. A Church in Agony   13

Chapter III. The Church and the
  Working-Man   28

Chapter IV. Disestablishment—The Story of
  à Bloodless Coup   37

Chapter V. The Use of Our Buildings   48

Chapter VI. The "Open Door" to a Secular
  Church   54

Chapter VII. The Secular Church –
  Apologia and Message   66

Chapter VIII. "To Proclaim the Gospel to
  the Poor"   87

Chapter IX. The Agape Supper—A Secular
  Communion   96

Chapter X. All Saints' Men's Club   109

Chapter XI. The Friendship Centre   116

Chapter XII. "Ahbenoojeyug"—The
  Canadian Indian Children's Programme   122

Chapter XIII. Dundas Day-Care—"Healing
    to them that are bruised"   129
Chapter XIV. Out of Christian Concern   136
Chapter XV. The Future of All Saints'   147
*Appendix: A Suggested Form of Service for
    the Lord's Supper*   154
Bibliography   159

AUTHOR'S NOTE

I desire to express my appreciation to the various leaders in and around All Saints' Church, Toronto, whose work makes up this story, and whose stories may add touches of reality. I would also like to express my thanks to the staff of General Publishing Company Limited, to Jack Stoddart, president, for his interest and kindness, and in particular to Pam Joho for her tremendous work and patience in editing the manuscript.

If this little book had a dedication, it would be to pals of mine like Don, Ed, Jerry and Harry, David and Happy, and a whole host of people who make life fun around All Saints', people who in a vast struggling sea of humanity are trying to keep their heads above water and to keep on striving for the shore, even picking up survivors on the way — and of course to those who are working to make this struggling sea eventually one of calm.

PROLOGUE

Of the old London during the Industrial Revolution, Charles Dickens wrote in *Dombey and Son:*

> The stragglers ... came wandering into London, by the great highway ..., footsore and weary, and gazing fearfully at the huge town before them ... Day after day, such travellers crept past, but always ... towards the town. Swallowed up in one phase or other of its immensity, towards which they seemed impelled by a desperate fascination, they never returned. Food for the hospitals, the churchyards, the prisons, the river, fever, madness, vice, and death – they passed on to the monster, roaring in the distance, and were lost.

Today one might stand at the corner of Sherbourne and Dundas streets in downtown Toronto, and see this very scene repeated in a city now expanding as the European cities did in the late nineteenth century. From the Maritimes, from northern Ontario, from the Indian reserves, from overseas, stragglers are drawn to the monster city, and they hardly ever return. Food for the hospital, the cemetery, the rooming-house, they are lost in the city, lost to their families, lost to society, lost almost to the human race, and certainly to the church.

The cry of this place rises to the skies; it screams with the wail of the siren; it moans with the sob of the drunk and the whine of the bum. The cry of this place rises to the heavens and it breaks the heart of God, for here daily on every street corner, in countless unknown lives, Christ is being crucified. Again, again, again, Calvary is being re-enacted here, half a mile from Yonge Street in the dropout area of the city.

This is Toronto's skid row, and at the throbbing heart of it stands a Christian church – at least we hope it is Christian, and that we have discarded some of the phony image that sticks fast as glue to such a middle-class institution. It is a supreme privilege for a church to be built in the centre of this place. Where anywhere could she better be? Where anywhere is a church needed more? For Christ is here so vividly in the suffering of men, women, and children; and where Christ is, there must His Church be. *Ubi Christus, ibi Ecclesia* – it is as simple as that.

The story I will try to tell is how this church – All Saints' Church, as stolid a church as Victorian, middle-class Protestant piety could make it – came to life in about the hundredth year of her existence. How a cold, barren refuge of the chosen few became a home for the city's multitudes. How from a holy club she became a church for the community. How in "disestablishment" she found new life. How, in ceasing to be a traditional "parish church", she became a true community parish. And how, in sharing the life-experience of Christ, she passed through the Cross to the light beyond.

We had so often read that a new kind of church, a church with a new look, was needed. So we made a new church: not by rebuilding but by refashioning. Despite the age of our church, we were able to start again. We rejected a pattern which came to us "ready-made", and we "tailor-made" a church to fit the needs of the people living around us, some of the poorest people in Canada.

I realize, of course, that the situation of All Saints' Church in Toronto is perhaps a peculiar one; not all churches have so exciting a locality – rather a wine-press than a vineyard! But from our happy experience we recommend throwing open a church to a swarming community. We recommend the way of self-abandonment, the jettisoning of so much that once seemed vital to the church, but which in a time or place of crisis is really excess baggage. We recommend secularizing the church itself, secularizing Christianity, for where is Christ but in the secular world, and where must His Church be but with Him in the secular world?

So we opened the doors of the church to let the captive Christ outside, or perhaps to let Him come in; and for almost the first time in our lives we feel we're doing the right thing in the right place at the right time. This is the story I try to tell, the message I try to bring, with the belief that what has been done in downtown Toronto can be equally well done (and why not better?) in Vancouver and Montreal, or for that matter in London, Liverpool, and Sheffield.

CHAPTER I
THE PLACE, THE PEOPLE

The face of my parish, if I may borrow an expression, has become ugly and blighted down the years. It is rapidly aging. It is pitted with the scars of empty lots. It is seamed with rows of ugly houses, and marked with the protuberances of high-rise buildings. Its profile shows decay, filth, abuse. Some features are beyond repair or the hope of a face-lift, while here and there, hastily applied makeup maintains a perpetual warfare with inner disintegration.

The boundaries of the area are Jarvis, Carlton, Parliament, and Queen East streets; this forms the parish of All Saints'. There are those who feel there is an intrinsic merit in some of the houses that remain here, but they must be possessed of a fascination for the ugly and the unbeautiful. Indeed, there are those who would preserve the thatched cottages of Merrie England or the dungeons of Edinburgh Castle, but we suggest that such places are better to visit than to inhabit. For good or bad, the inner city of Toronto missed the air raids which removed so many of the slums in European cities, thereby giving them the chance of a new start. But some reformers have suggested a strategic air raid in Toronto's skid row, or at least a careful disposition of delayed-action blockbuster land-mines (residents would of course be informed beforehand, with a few notable exceptions we might suggest at City Hall!). With the future of the district in the balance, the debate goes on between community workers, developers, politicians, concerned people, and still others who want to make the place "safe" for the middle class. For even this area is becoming too expensive a place for poor people to live.

We enter in imagination at Jarvis Street; it is well that we keep together if it is after dark. Jarvis Street possesses most of the institutions which make men go astray, and at the same time most of the institutions which desperately attempt to bring them back to the straight and narrow path – rather like an expensive drugstore which sells on one counter tobacco and on another medicine to stop people from smoking. Generally speaking, this is a residential district, perhaps the nearest one of such dimensions to the centre of the city. There are still a few good houses left, remnants of old homes now turned into rooming-houses in which a number of men have rooms, sharing sometimes the same bathroom and the same bottle. In distinct contrast to this are a number of cottages of the one-storey type, frame buildings of the sort we are used to seeing on the edge of most Ontario towns and villages. Here they remain in the heart of a modern city, occupying valuable space, old-fashioned, uncomfortable, needing repair. Shall we pull them down, or wait till they fall down themselves? There are also quite a few small stores that some of us have known since childhood, and a certain amount of industry – nightclubs, hostels, flophouses, the Warwick and Westover Hotels with their garish posters, a few pubs.

In stark contrast, and in increasing numbers, are the high-rise apartment buildings – Moss Park Housing, originally low rental but now Ontario Housing, Bradwin Court, the first high-rise rooming-house in Canada, and others presently under construction. It is in high-rise buildings, sociologists tell us, that the future criminals of the nation are being nourished and brought up. Yet I personally have found a pretty happy atmosphere in those high-rises I know, and a pretty good group of people – some a little rough, of course, some out of work, some very commendable families who have waited a long time to move here, some elderly people who are so happy to be paying only $31 a month here instead of $12 to $15 a week for some bug-ridden apartment in a rooming-house. At least there is a measure of privacy in a high-rise apartment building; privacy is so often lacking in the large older house that has been converted into as many apartments as possible. High-rise Ontario Housing may not be heaven on earth, but some of the old rooming-houses are pretty near hell.

What of the people living in this area? They are of almost every type and from almost everywhere under the sun. We must realize that in our ministry we tend to meet more of the noisy, obstreperous folks than the quiet and law-abiding; we may notice one drunk for ten sober, one disturbed for ten normal people. Having said that, it must be admitted that a large number of the residents and transients are, in some way or another, sick. One recent study of the area south of Carlton revealed that the death-rate was far higher here than in any other part of Toronto; this was especially true of infant mortality and of death from alcoholism.

Many of the people here are ugly to the point of deformity. Dejection, often verging on despair, is clearly expressed on the faces of both men and women. There are many scrawny, scraggy children, and just as many who are fat from bad feeding. The number of obvious alcoholics is appalling. At the corner of Sherbourne and Dundas streets on a Sunday morning – Sunday, when the missions are closed, is the bad day of the week on skid row – you may see twenty or thirty men hanging around with nowhere to go and all the time in the world to go there. Many young women have come to look about twice their age because they are too poor or too disinterested to replace teeth they have lost through neglect, improper nourishment, or just too many children.

Faces, faces – and despair or depression visible in nearly every one of them. The transient rooting in the garbage can to dig out the daily paper: the scrounger going from mission to mission with his or her paper bag; the jovial character wheeling home on "cheque-day" with his "pleasure-pak", his "big ale in the big land", who will live like a king for a day or two – of course, the TV commercials don't show his lousy little $12 room in this "big land", or the condition of his liver. And everybody wearing clothes that have belonged to someone else, out of fashion, the wrong size, because on welfare he can't afford to buy clothes of his own. So what Forest Hill wears today, skid row will wear a few years from now. If it wasn't for the clothing missions, half the population would be half-naked. Why, put out a little stock of gloves on a cold day: the men will grab them like children fighting for candy.

Where do these people come from? Just as people poured in from every village and town to the old cities of the Industrial Revolution, so now they pour in from the surrounding country to Toronto, from the east, from the west, from the north, from any place you can think of. Apart from the older residents, very few are Torontonians. Most old Toronto natives have made good and moved out of the area; a few elderly people have got kind of stuck here and are now afraid to move, yet they are not really at home any longer. Folks come down here to make a start. If they have any "get up and go", that is precisely what they do – move out, into Ontario Housing, which is the dream of nearly every family, for there is almost nowhere else they can go. But some stay and sink to the level of the Anglo-Saxon skid row – for nearly all the alcoholics here are of British origin with good English names.[1] It takes God's Englishmen, Irishmen, and Scotsmen to make our best drunks (though not the Welshmen: they love their country too much to leave it for Toronto).

By far the largest element of the population, and the most noticeable, are unemployed, middle-aged men. They look older than they are. Weatherbeaten, prematurely grey, they are easily discernible in their out-of-date clothing, a clever blend of

[1] Only 20% are real alcoholics, but many more are drinkers, according to the Rev. Bruce Howe in his report *Single Displaced Persons in Downtown Toronto* (1972). He also adds that 22% come from the Maritimes, 47.3% from Ontario, and 16.7% from overseas – this based on an enquiry of 443 men in the local missions and drop-in centres.

Ivy League and Salvation Army. Most have a disability, natural and chronic, sometimes caused by excessive drinking.

There are twelve thousand such men in the city, and several thousand live and move within this area alone. And each costs the city several thousand dollars a year. Some have left their families miles and years ago. Some will have a relative, a sister in Scarborough, though they "don't bother" with one another. Of course, these men live at different levels. Some sleep outside, or in the railway station. Others live purely to drink; the "winos", they will drink anywhere, up any back alley, even behind a buttress of the church, and are temporarily lost to humanity like the brickmakers in Dickens' *Bleak House*. Some have binges when they are flush with money; they drink furiously; they eat almost nothing. Others live a life of alternating sobriety and drunkenness. Some struggle bravely; most fail till it breaks their hearts and the hearts of those who love and care for them. A few win, come out on top, but others drink themselves to death, and have an unknown funeral with not one relative or friend at the graveside.

Most of these men are unemployed because they are, or have become, unemployable. It's hard to get a regular job if your address is the Men's Hostel at Seaton House or one of the missions. Yet many of them are very likable, generous, would share their last drink or smoke. Some are very silent. Others talk of better days, occasionally even of a college education. Some speak of their wives and families, but many have suffered tragedies, like one man I met who had lost two children in two separate car accidents, or another whose wife and children were burnt to death while he was at Mass on Christmas Eve. Many have just not got what it takes to stay alive and out of prison in this complex struggle for existence, which we flatter by calling a democracy or the world of private enterprise.

Where do they live? Anywhere, some would say, or nowhere. Most live in rooms of varying quality, and are continually moving. In and out of the Seaton House hostel, where the staff do their best to do an impossibly hard job, or in and out of missions like the Salvation Army or Fred Victor. And some few live in the "revolving door": first in jail, then at the detox (detoxification centre), the hostel, the rooming-house while they have some kind of a job that brings in a little money, and then, after they begin drinking again, back to jail or the detox, where the sad dehumanizing process begins all over again. Yet, as Dr. E. Mansell Pattison, an associate professor of psychiatry and human behaviour at the University of California, has noted in a recent article in the Addiction Research Foundation's *Journal*:

> The skid row habitué, though he may use or abuse alcohol, is not primarily an alcoholic.... Typically, he is a socially inept individual with minimal ego coping skills, who has always operated on the marginal edge of society. The "revolving door" police court system, the flophouse hostel, the Salvation Army centre, the jail, the work farm, and the other skid row facilities essentially offer this marginal man of society the same simple things: shelter, warmth, a bit of quiet and repose. To speak of rehabilitation in this situation is a misnomer, for these people have never achieved primary socialization.

So there is no simple answer to the question of rehabilitation, for most of these men have known no settled life to be rehabilitated to.

The place, the whole place, is wicked, you might say, as wicked as hell. But most of all it is sick. And it is sad, very sad, for in the midst of all, in the heart of skid row, is Christ, the Man of Nazareth, the Friend of man, Whose heart is very sad.

CHAPTER II
A CHURCH IN AGONY

On one of the more fashionable corners of Toronto's skid row – Sherbourne and Dundas streets – there stands the once-proud Church of All Saints'. She looks rather forlorn, with something of the air of a dowager duchess maintaining a relic of grandeur and dignity, but perhaps a little seedy and faded round the edges, as she nears her hundredth year. Her only remaining wealth lies in the value of her property.

The parish history began in 1872, when a group of people in a new residential area of the city saw the need for a church to serve this eastern section of Toronto, at that time a city of 75,000 souls. A site was purchased for $2,200 at the corner of Sherbourne and Beech Street (later renamed Wilton Avenue and still later Dundas Street East). A modest wooden church was built and opened by Bishop Bethune on Sunday, 16 June 1872. This first small church soon became inadequate for a growing congregation, however, and the present church was built at a cost of $15,000 and opened on Sunday, 29 November 1874. It was built to the glory of God and in affectionate remembrance of

Queen Victoria, and dedicated in the name of All Saints', with special preference given to those of middle-class background and definitely Protestant leanings!

The history of All Saints' has been quite illustrious. Great names in Toronto and in Canada have been associated with her: the Hon. G. W. Allan, Sir Charles Tupper, the Hon. John A. Macdonald, Sir Alexander Campbell, the Galts, as well as a number of noted brewers (an industry on which the Anglican Church has been floated somewhat unsteadily on two continents). While the area remained middle-class, the congregation filled a church which seated 800 people. All Saints' Sunday school had 1,500 scholars. Her lacrosse and soccer teams won championships. She had her own missionary in China. She contributed to the building of other churches.

In the years of the Depression and the Second World War, the middle class were moving out to the suburbs. All Saints' now experienced the lot of numerous churches in European and North American cities – a large church building housed a small congregation. For some years the church piously, if ineffectively and somewhat purposelessly, struggled and no doubt prayed to preserve something that the local working-class population did not really want. Meanwhile, like colonists, the members of the congregation would come down Sunday by Sunday from the suburbs. They dearly loved their old church in this rapidly deteriorating neighbourhood, but would hurry back again from streets that had become foreign, and from a population that had become strange, if not repulsive. In other words, there was no longer much involvement with

the people for whom the church had been built to
serve, namely the local people, the real parishioners. For be assured, in the true Anglican tradition
"parish" means the local community, and the parishioners are the bodies and souls in that area
for whom the ministry of the local church is responsible.

I pause to wonder why it is that the former
members of a church continue to haunt their old
ecclesiastical preserve. It is good and noble in one
sense, no doubt, and very natural. But how terrible
it is when a group of former parishioners continue
to come to a parish with which they are growing
more and more out of touch, fight with the fury of
the devil to go on governing their old church, and
then have the effrontery to complain that the local
people don't come and are no longer interested in
"church". This paternalism, a sort of "white
father" attitude, still remains in many of our city
churches, and it is the ruin of them. Of course,
sometimes these people are doing their best according to their own light. How often, though, how
very often the light of one generation has proved
to be darkness to the next. And meanwhile the
outside world sees us as a tired little bunch of
people who shelter within the walls of shabby
buildings, struggling just to keep ourselves alive,
when we should be the life-givers of the whole
community. So the world that always suspected the
church was phony is ultimately convinced that we
really are.

It was to this typical downtown church set-up
that I came in September 1964. The church "living" had actually been vacant for nine months, and
had been well eschewed by the local clergy, who,

"wiser in their generation", had resisted all attempts to be drawn into possession. At last, in desperation, the congregation began to look farther afield, and it was then, I sometimes say, that they found a clown like me to come. I had been buried in the hinterland – twelve years in Huron's green and pleasant land. I used to pray that the world would stop and give me a chance to jump back on again. Then my prayer was answered. It stopped, I jumped, I crash-landed on skid row.

I can well remember the ghastly feeling as I first saw the drab-looking pile, with its wall-to-wall pews and its altar all draped with funeral shrouds, to preserve it for the following Sunday. I was led in solemn state through one building after another, each more cheerless than the last, till finally we came to the ultimate disaster area, the gymnasium. Here the church notice-board bore a fitting caption: THE WAGES OF SIN IS DEATH . . . EVERYBODY WELCOME. And the outside was even more grim than the interior – black as Hades with the grime of ninety years. I remembered the Assyrian song about the underworld: "Dust lies thick on bolt and door." You could pass this building at night and know you had gone by something dark.

I was not surprised that, with the church buildings so drab, the church people were not exactly a fun-crowd or an ecclesiastical jet-set. All of us tend to mourn the passing of that kind of religion we are brought up in – in this case a Protestantism which finds duty rather than love in religion. And these people, poor souls, were mostly too old to adapt to a new situation; their theology had been taught them fifty years earlier by a clergy who had learned their theology fifty years before that. They could have no feeling that the church should be adapted to the local needs, no feeling that the church really exists for those who do not belong to it, no feeling that there could be any form of Christianity but their own. Still, they would complain: "We offer the church services and the people don't come; they just don't care about God any more." And nothing the Archangel Gabriel could do would change the thinking of these people.

For the first two years of my ministry, 1964-6, I made a general effort to run the church and parish much as any other parish. I concentrated on building the congregational life (I had been told I was hired to build up the congregation!). There was a great deal of pastoral visiting, especially in the Moss Park Ontario Housing complex, where two thousand people lived. In their grounds north of Queen Street we put on what we claim to be the first outdoor Christmas nativity play in Canada. We formed children's groups, especially a junior choir which we rounded up in the manner of an English pressgang (except that unfortunately they could take shore-leave when they wished). There was also a continual concern for social work and outreach, although this was not at first greatly emphasized.

A fair measure of success was attained; the congregation grew somewhat, despite the religious depression of the sixties, and we began to have our first faltering thoughts about improving the church buildings. A visitation of our parish was conducted by thirty men of the Brotherhood of Anglican Churchmen and of the Lay Readers' Association, and we formed friendships with other churches, which were later to revolutionize our whole ministry. For example, an offer came from St. George's parish (Islington) to support us in various ways: this offer was presented to the Urban Archdeacon, the wardens and the vestry, or governing body. Although some of the officials expressed opposition, they were compelled by the vestry to accept, and eventually St. George's took over our Sunday school.

At another meeting the officials effectively opposed the employment of a boys' worker, and refused to accept a resolution that money from the Synod (which included investment and interest) be used for this and similar needs. Obviously, a state of conflict was developing, as I noted at the time:

> The feeling of the rector is that the officials are doing their best, consciously or unconsciously, to halt the forward march of the church. The rector and several members of the Board see this as a day of great opportunity, with the coming growth of the parish, and are distressed by the repellent appearance of the church. The rector feels strongly that no real mission can go forward while the church looks as it does. He feels that the present policy is delaying progress and burying the church. There is $25,000 that might be spent on church repair, but the cry of the wardens is that without the interest on that money we cannot survive. The opinion of the rector is that survival under the present terms is worse than death. He therefore seeks the opinion of the Bishop as to whether he should fight for a new and greater ministry, or whether he should resign and let the wardens carry on in their own sweet and aimless manner.

Needless to say, from this time on there was continual friction between myself (and those who supported me) and the more conservative members.

The object of the latter group seemed to be to hang on and preserve a ministry in the church, even though it was quite unimaginative, out of touch with all modern progress, and equally out of touch with the needs of the community. The issue centred largely around money – whether to jog along on the interest accruing on the thirty or forty thousand dollars invested with the Synod, or whether to "blow" a few thousand to make the church presentable and to adopt a more aggressive ministry that might be worth preserving. I frequently reminded myself of the parable of the fig-tree, which grew leaves but produced no fruit: why let it cumber the earth?

The battle continued, but gradually certain victories were won. By now St. George's Church ran a successful Sunday school in our parish. Consent was finally given for a good deal of work on the church; much enthusiasm was engendered and the wardens themselves began to take the lead. A few pews at the back of the church (about five feet from the doors) were removed to create a narthex or vestibule. Most conspicuous of all, the interior of the Parish Hall and the exterior of the church were sandblasted – a remarkable face-lift! In a few hours the dirt and grime of ages was removed, the whole front of the church ceased to be black, and became bright yellow with red facings. We had had no idea that there was so much colour. A sense of shock pervaded the neighbourhood as people noticed a bright church building at the corner of the street which seemed to have sprung up overnight. One or two streetcars missed their usual landmark for a stopping place. Drunks coming home late, or rather early in the morning, from local nightclubs were quite baffled. A well-known landmark was gone, and in its place was something new.

By this time – toward the end of 1967 – I felt I had begun to get the hang of things, a feeling for the neighbourhood and some sense of direction. My first year or two had been largely a matter of sorting things out, and getting to know a new population – a time of relying on unreliable people, of intense visiting, of beginning new organizations and fostering their growth, of seeking for leaders, of making false starts. It had been a time of alternating doubt and disappointment, hope and desperation, and frustration at the obstacles and inadequacies. At last, however, a fairly clear picture of my ministry had taken shape. It would involve a three-fold thrust of pastoral, evangelistic, and outreach ministry (this last a ministry to those completely outside the church at all).

The church was at this time operating in low key with a congregation of from seventy to ninety people. The core-members were the older people who had moved away from the district; but the majority lived fairly near – if not actually in – the parish, coming largely from the Moss Park complex, with just a few from the older part of the parish. I was conscious of the tremendous ministry required, and of the great opportunity the Church of Christ possessed in having this bridgehead in the heart of alien territory.

But how great was the need for manpower, resources, money! Compelled to look beyond the parish for resources of manpower, I appealed to the Bishop, to other authorities, to friendly churches, to diocesan groups:

We are too few, the congregation is too old, too lacking in resources, to do the job that must be done. It is a mission that is greater than All Saints': it is the true concern of the whole Church . . . It is still possible that the inner city can be saved for the Anglican Church. Can we expect an elderly and rather uneducated congregation to be responsible for so great a task? Can we expect a few old ladies to finance a mission to the inner city? It is therefore without any feeling of guilt, without reserve, that we seek aid, for it is not for ourselves, not for the survival of All Saints', but that we may fulfil the charge committed to us (clergy and congregation), as in the immortal words: "Receive this charge, thy care and mine."

To me this is an extension parish, very truly, for the houses will be new and the people will be new, as though another town is being built around an old village church. I look at my job partly as funnelling resources into this scene of operation (as do our missionary bishops in their dioceses). So we look for friends of All Saints' and of the inner city. Perhaps we might be so bold as to wonder if a group of men and women, at the call of the Bishop, would dedicate themselves to work in downtown Toronto . . . and be actively involved in the local church. We can, of course, jog along and keep the old place going, especially if we shut ourselves off from the community – or, with help, we can do a real job. This is the present crisis of All Saints', but I believe it is a crisis which might be an opportunity for the Church at large.

Here was born the idea of the "Friends of All Saints'", a group which was ultimately to be our salvation, as I will describe in a later chapter. The mission and the ministry widened rather slowly in the next two years or so. It was a period of tension and of finding the way; as we were to realize later, we were moving towards a time of decision.

Then, dramatically and unexpectedly, there was a new phase. From the diocese came a proposal to amalgamate the parish of St. Bartholomew on Dundas Street East with the parish of All Saints' (the two churches were only 1,700 feet apart), then sell the site of All Saints', take down the rather old St. Bart's buildings, and build a new fine church and community hall on an extended St. Bart's site! It looked so sensible on paper, and diocesan committees love paper. The proposal was pushed hard, and was readily accepted by St. Bart's, who had everything to gain; but it was rejected by All Saints', who had everything to lose. On this occasion I found myself aligned with the wardens and rejoiced in their obduracy. I thought that each parish needed a full-time ministry. The two were so different: St. Bart's was the new-housing area of Regent Park, virulent and tough, but All Saints' was the dying, drop-out, skid row area. I could see in the proposal no consideration being given to the thousands of needy people in the All Saints' neighbourhood, a neighbourhood in which there was no other church near by for poor people who did not possess cars, who had to think twice about streetcar fares, and who seldom went more than two or three blocks from their homes. The proposal seemed to be leaving our area unprotected, by giving up a place in an area of the city where a real church ministry was most needed. So ultimately the proposal was rejected, though we lost a few friends at headquarters.

But this "escape" did not give us a feeling of contentment. Arguments about the future went on, and were not allowed to die down. I renewed the attack, warning the congregation that, although for a time the heat from the diocese was turned off, we would not be allowed to rest in peace for long, nor could we cut down our commitments. "I can think of nothing more depressing, less Christian, than any such idea of coasting along," I told them. "I have fought together with you against what I thought was not a good resolution by the Urban Board, but I will fight a lot harder against such a policy as this. I would personally have no interest in a church which adopted such a line."

The next suggestion for development was to build a high-rise complex on the site of the present church, with the church on the ground floor and, if possible, appropriate offices, halls, and space for medical, psychiatric, and legal aid, as well as for the general care of the community. A meeting was engineered between some of the Friends of All Saints' (many of them well-disposed businessmen) and a local firm of developers; a good deal of thought was given to the idea, and hopes rose fairly high. Here was something exciting that would make use of the one thing we possessed – our property. Here perhaps would be a first for the Anglican Church in Canada. It was to remain only a dream, however, and the greatest dreamer was to find that he was not without honour save in his own denomination. Rightly or wrongly, the diocesan authorities were concerned over the mode of financing: the church board was frightened; the idea was too new and revolutionary. The developers, who were the most optimistic, soon saw that there was little hope.

After this, matters bumbled along for a little while, as a sense of insecurity depressed and perhaps diminished the congregation. However, the power of the church leaders was gradually decreasing in various ways, while the influence of the Friends of All Saints' was increasing, and even being felt in some of our planning meetings. Now arose a third plan, for which my own open mind and still more open mouth were chiefly responsible! After a visit to St. Luke's United Church (our neighbours at Carlton and Sherbourne streets), I suggested the physical union of St. Luke's and All Saints'. The area of work in the two parishes was almost identical; theology and outlook were alike. Why not bring the congregation of All Saints' to St. Luke's, where a good-sized chapel would be at their convenience for public worship? At the same time, both Anglican and United would work together in the field of social service and Christian outreach.

Synod and Conference lapped up the idea: the breeze of ecumenism was blowing strongly at the moment, and the scheme struck a congenial note – it would look fine in the press. The United Church authorities and the congregation of St. Luke's were delighted by the prospect, and most gracious in welcoming our approach; they had combined three congregations of their own into one West Don Parish, and now All Saints' could be a fourth member of the combine. Frequent meetings were held, the bishops were on our side, and the Synod authorities were excited. All Saints' would be demolished; a small building would perhaps be set up as a House Church on or near the site of All Saints' (unfortunately, the authorities never gave any assurance of this). Thus free of cumbersome buildings, free of so much worry, and with the interest from a valuable property sale, the ministry of the true Church – a ministry to people – would be gloriously equipped for action.

But at this point I was faced with a few questions: How did I feel about taking down a fine old church? How did I feel about being a preacher without a pulpit, a sort of minister without portfolio? While expressing a natural regret at the thought of tearing down a fine set of church buildings, I could not but feel a sense of relief: in this Anglo-Saxon ghetto the need was for a practical building rather than a Gothic structure. We needed a place, not so much to which we could say "come", but from which a few of us would go. A perfectly valid ministry could carry on without any large home-base, by going to high-rise apartments, Seaton House Men's Hostel, the hospitals, the homes of the people ... Would such an action of abandonment denote failure? Only, I believe, in the sense that Christ was a failure. We might have failed here in the slums to build a middle-class congregation; but what we now needed was to form a community of the poor, the destitute, the alcoholic, the prostitute. When the Children of Israel were in the desert, an overshadowing cloud represented the Lord's presence, and they were instructed to move on or stay in camp according to whether the cloud moved or stayed. It seems that the cloud of the Lord's presence has moved from so many of our churches, while we have stayed behind in the camp. Perhaps here we had the chance to form a pilgrim church, not a static organization, but one like the people of Israel on the march, dwelling in tents, not temples – which is the Biblical conception of the Church in both the Old and the New Testaments. So a note of "kenosis", the spirit of self-abandonment or self-emptying of Philippians II, entered in, a note that would be heard loud and clear in the rest of our story. This self-immolation of a church would be a little like sharing the Cross of Jesus of Nazareth – dying to live, the resurrection, the phoenix.

It was time to present this plan for a union of All Saints' and St. Luke's to the vestry, or general meeting. Here – rather surprisingly – came disaster. The resolution to demolish All Saints' buildings and remove the congregation to St. Luke's had been carefully thought out, and was powerfully supported and well-presented by the Assistant Bishop Garnsworthy in person – but it was turned down. Only narrowly, by just a few votes, and those chiefly from people who hardly came to church at all. This little group of people unexpectedly turned the issue. The decision was received with dismay and surprise by many, including the Bishop, and also our friends of the United Church. It appeared to be the final act of obstinacy, the last kick in the face of the Synod authorities. At a meeting of the Executive Committee of the Synod, the Bishop was given authority to disestablish All Saints' at his discretion. We waited daily for the axe to fall, and I took a sudden interest in vacant rectories!

But nothing happened. Summer came, and we received a request from the "Friendship Centre", a large men's club and coffee-house that had formerly been meeting in a disused pub, to use the Parish Hall most afternoons and evenings. About the same time, too, a pious hope of mine came alive: a clinic from Queen Street Mental Health Hospital, a kind of halfway house operation, moved into the gymnasium and the Baldwin Hall. All Saints' was beginning to find a ministry of outreach; she and her big buildings might be needed. We had always felt that there was need for a very vital ministry in this part of the city – not perhaps the type of ministry that we had been offering, the traditional church of religion only, but a true church ministry to people. Before, we had been too few to cope with the huge demands that would be made upon a really live Christian ministry on skid row. Now here were men and women of goodwill, skilled and enthusiastic, not necessarily Anglicans, not necessarily religious people, but obviously moved and inspired by the God of Love. We would welcome these people to care for the community from underneath our roof, and do what we were too few or too inexpert to do ourselves. Thus there might be as many as forty fully-paid social workers employed at one time in the service of the community, working in and out of our church buildings.

Here, finally, was a beginning of hope for All Saints'. Here at last was opportunity. We had been thinking of tearing down the church buildings; now everyone seemed to want them, anxious to use them for community purposes. Indeed, our large buildings had suddenly become a point of strength.

CHAPTER III

THE CHURCH AND THE WORKING-MAN

We stood poised to leap, to launch out into a new ministry. It seemed appropriate to pause a moment to catch our breath, to make a few discoveries, to think about where we were.

About this time I was beginning to read, quite furiously, a good many books that I should have read before. This reading greatly clarified for me the whole picture of the ministry of a Christian church, and also of the sphere in which my sort of church was operating. A great truth now broke upon me, something I had inarticulately felt during my city ministry in England, something which had been faintly dawning in my new ministry in Toronto. It is this: *The urban masses do not go to church*. The working-class, the "blue-collar" workers, the poorer people, the unemployed, do not go to church; and they have never done so, in any general way, since cities began. This truth dawned on me from out of a dark and foreboding sky.

Previously, when I had considered our failure to relate as a worshipping people to the masses around us, it had seemed that in my particular case one or more things must be wrong: (1) the people of my parish must be very bad, since almost none come to church; (2) I must be a very bad minister not to do better; and (3) our church itself must be very ineffective. I was now to realize, however, what must be a tremendous relief to many of the inner-city clergy of Britain, Europe, and North America – that this is the case almost everywhere, and always has been. It is not that the people are necessarily wicked because they do not come to church; it isn't that the clergy are especially bad in the inner city; it isn't that the churches are particularly ineffective. It is just that poor people do not generally go to the middle-class church, or belong to the cultural setting which the middle-class church (especially the more established Protestant groups) provides.

If I seem to labour this point, it is because it is not readily accepted by many authorities or by those who are not closely involved. Yet it is the incontrovertible finding of history and sociology in Britain, Europe (especially France and West Germany), and more recently North America. "It is not that the Church has lost the great towns; it has never had them," wrote a notable English bishop of the late Victorian era.[1] And when Archbishop Longley remarked, "The Church has lost the towns," Disraeli is reported to have replied, "Your Grace is mistaken; the Church never had the towns." This is the blunt truth of history: the poorer people in cities never went to church.

During the Industrial Revolution in Britain and much of Europe, a migrant population flooded into

[1] A. F. Winnington-Ingram, *Work in Great Cities* (London, 1896), p. 2.

the cities from the rural areas. Many of these
people had been church-goers when they wore their
farmers' smocks; they attended church fairly regularly under the watchful eye of the village squire.
But when they got to London, and exchanged the
smock for a black suit, they gave up church-going
right away. There seems to have been no bridge
between the church-going villager of Jane Austen's
rural England and the pagan townsman of Dickens' London.

The conditions in cities were, of course, appalling. The inhabitants were brutalized, and so intent
on earning a living – or an existence – that they had
little time to think of religion. Work was so hard,
and the hours so long, that they were too tired to
go to church. If they did make the effort, they had
to wait outside till the "quality" had come in and
occupied the pews which they rented. After this a
few of the poor might be admitted to some miserable free sittings in the cheaper places or in the
aisles. (In Sheffield in 1821, with a population of
60,000, there were not more than 300 free sittings
for the poor in all the "established" churches.[2]) It
is no wonder that Pusey speaks of the alleys of
London where the gospel was as unknown as in
Tibet.

As a result the Church, anxious and concerned,
set about building many new churches in the
poorer parts of the cities. These were intended
particularly for the local neighbourhoods, but generally the poor did not attend them. As a character
says in Charles Kingsley's *Yeast* (1849):

After all the expense, when they've built the

---

[2] Edward R. Wickham, *Church and People in an Industrial City*
(London: Lutterworth Press, 1957), p. 70.

church, it's the trademen and the gentry, and the old folk, that fill it, and the working-man never comes near it from one year's end to another.

K. S. Inglis, in his study of the church and the working-class in Victorian England, supports the view that the new churches were half-empty and not attended by the poor.[3] Owen Chadwick quotes the famous Mann's Census of 1851, which indicated that 58% of the population attended church, and which suggested reasons why the other 5½ million – the labouring myriads – stayed away:

> They dislike the social distinction in churches, the division into respectable pews and free seats, and regard religion as a middle-class propriety or luxury, suspect the churches of being indifferent to their poverty, and think that the message of the clergy is vitiated because they were paid to deliver it. They live in such physical squalor that they cannot rise to the things of the spirit. The number of ministers at present is too few to reach them.[4]

Other historians record the lack of concern, and sometimes the actual disfavour, with which the established church looked at the rise of farmers' unions and labour unions in England. In a country destined to rise to socialism, the church (often known as the Conservative Party at Prayer) quite obviously backed the wrong horse! Nor were the other denominations much more successful than the Church of England. The Roman Catholic Church was strengthened by poor Irish immigrants, and the Primitive Methodists and Salvation Army

---

[3] K. S. Inglis, *Churches and the Working Classes in Victorian England* (London: Routledge, Kegan Paul; and Toronto: University of Toronto Press, 1963), p. 60.

[4] Owen Chadwick, *The Victorian Church*, Part I (London: A. & C. Black, 1966-70), p. 366.

probably did a little better, but in time these latter converts became respectable and therefore middle-class, and were lost to their own society.

Of the church in modern England much has been written. I quote only an English cleric who was appointed to make a study of the riverside and inner-city parishes of the Southwark diocese (generally Southeast London). The similarity of this minister's conclusions and my own drawn from my ministry in both Liverpool and Toronto is remarkable. He writes in a memorandum:

> I have investigated in every way that I could – history, sociology, the life of this church and that – the inner-city situation of the Church, and I know now for certain ... *the Church never had the working-class* ... The working-man would do almost anything for a vicar who is "good to them" except come to church regularly ... I am surrounded by three blocks of working-class tenements ... I have got to know a good many of the inhabitants on "chatty terms". I *know* that in my life-time none of them is likely to be a regular church-goer ... There are *some* middle-class people in the parish – a handful. I should not be surprised to find one or two of them getting caught up with the church – but they will almost certainly move away when they can. Anyone who gets on, gets out.[5]

For northwestern Europe the case is presented in a work by Horst Symanowski, an industrial pastor in West Germany. Robert Starbuck, who wrote the introduction to Symanowski's book, tells us that only 5% of the population attend church, and only 1% of the industrial working-class. He contrasts

---

[5] Rev. Eric James, *Memorandum to the Bishop of Southwark, on the Church in the Inner City.*

this with the countries behind the Iron Curtain, where he says that from 25% to 30% attend church.[6] And the French proletariate, according to Abbé Godin, is completely apart from a church which has an entirely bourgeois outlook and mentality. Another French writer points out that the proletariate have either deserted the churches or else, by staying in the churches, have deserted their class.

Moving to the American scene, we find the situation somewhat different, but of course the industrial workers there have been in a better income-bracket for some time, while the poorer masses are still somewhat inarticulate and without a strong political party. Starbuck writes:

> It would seem that the only modern industrial nation in the western world where a large segment of the population regularly participates in the church is the astonishingly "churchy" U.S.A. There are no doubt reasons for the abnormal situation of the churches here, but there are many signs that it may become much more "normal" in the not too far distant future. . . . Beneath the surface of American churchiness one senses the same profound estrangement of the church from the secular world here as in Europe.[7]

The Bishop of Indianapolis, in his book *The Church Reclaims the City*, suggests that the break of the working-classes from the church in the United States is only "slightly delayed",[8] while Harvey Cox explains in *The Secular City* that the

---

[6] Robert B. Starbuck, in his introduction to Horst Symanowski's *The Christian Witness in an Industrial Society*, translated by George H. Kehm (Philadelphia: Westminster Press, 1964), p. 12.

[7] Ibid., p. 13.

[8] Paul Moore, Jr., *The Church Reclaims the City* (New York: Seabury Press, 1964), p. 20.

traditional parish is completely out of place in the metropolis.[9] With its great emphasis on the small local community, pot-luck suppers, church bazaars, and so on, the parish is effective in small towns, but not so happily placed in a technopolis.

In Canada there has always been a strong church life (of a more Irish-Scottish than Anglo-Saxon type, I personally think). But the tremendous growth of the cities in the last thirty years, the present immigration from the less "churchy" countries of Europe, and the numbers of families pouring into the cities from the rural areas and small towns have quite definitely changed the picture. Nor has the religious depression of recent years helped a great deal.

In a recent report on church attendance given by the Downtown Church Workers' Association in Toronto, figures revealed that, of the vast population south of Wellesley Street, about 300 to 400 people go to ten local Anglican churches.[10] This means that in each congregation only about thirty to forty people come to church from their own parish (using the word "parish" in its geographical sense). The rest of the congregation is coming from elsewhere. Many of the local parishioners are older and retired people, university students, and children; so how many working-men in this area of downtown Toronto go to church?

Edward Wickham, Bishop of Middleton, Manchester, in a careful study of the Church in industrial areas, reminds us that the working-class

---

[9] Harvey Cox, *The Secular City* (New York: Macmillan, 1965), chapter 2 *passim*, p. 70.

[10] Prof. S. Crysdale, *Report to the Downtown Church Workers' Association of the Diocese of Toronto* (July 1970).

who live downtown gradually move out into the suburban areas, and they usually bring with them their habits of poor church-attendance.[11] So the inner suburbs are thus becoming afflicted with the same problems as the downtown churches. Generally, the inner-city churches struggle, the inner-suburban churches labour, and the farther-off suburban churches, which attract white-collar people, thrive.

My aim in this chapter has not been to be deliberately depressing. I have used the "loud pedal" because so many people will not accept what I am trying to say. It is that both history and experience have shown that the church organization is generally the possession of the middle class, the clerical and professional people, and that the humble masses of the city, workers or unemployed, are almost entirely out of touch with the church as we know it.

So what do we do with a poor industrial parish? What do we do with the church? Here we are at All Saints' with a large, really poor population, not even working-class but rather unworking. We have a huge, even magnificent church, but this has not drawn the people, and has almost repelled them. For my people are afraid of organized religion; they tend to be suspicious of what they see of churches. Our Prayer Book and liturgy is no doubt incomparable, but to them it is also incomprehensible. (People in the back-streets find references to Og the king of Bashan entirely irrelevant to their daily life; Sihon King of the Amorites leaves them cold.) Even the Bible needs too much explaining

---

[11] Edward R. Wickham, *Church and People in an Industrial City*, chapter 5.

and translating, save for such local translations as the Liverpool "Scouse" version.

Our main duty is to propagate the gospel. Where the church organization has failed to do this among the poor, we must seek other ways. This, I believe, is the greatest issue facing the home church today. Where people cannot understand or relate to our services, we must produce something simple and meaningful to them. Where they do not receive the sacrament of the Communion because they "stumble" at the church door, we must offer the sacrament in their apartments or in the Parish Hall. We must take the gospel to people where they are – where Christ probably is, too. And there we will find – or found – a Church. For the true Church is not necessarily buildings or an organization but a few people dedicated in the Name of Christ.

This, I finally concluded, must be part of our ministry at All Saints'. This we would attempt, with the encouragement of a bishop who said he would welcome any reasonable experiment, even if it turned out to be wrong, rather than go on doing the same ineffective things for ever.

CHAPTER IV

DISESTABLISHMENT – THE STORY OF A BLOODLESS COUP

In the fall and winter of 1970, church-life at All Saints' was quite active – at least in the field of social Christianity. The Friendship Centre, opened that summer, was daily bringing hundreds of men into the Parish Hall. The new Mental Health After-Care program was operating strongly. There was legal-aid counselling given by law students, contact with Canadian Indian agencies, and a quite active Men's Club.

But the whole management of the church was extremely shaky. There was no real leadership; business administration was far from adequate. In desperation, and alarmed at the possibility of complete disintegration, I called together the little group I mentioned earlier, the Friends of All Saints'. These were about half a dozen business-men, members of other congregations (mostly, as it happened, associated with "Tuesday on the Square" of Holy Trinity Church) who had for some years been interested in the cause of All Saints'. With these men I had been meeting for lunch each month, and they probably preserved my sanity. They were all leaders in their own fields:

one the chairman of the Church of the Good Samaritan (a men's home), another chairman of St. Leonard's House, also a church warden, and a secretary of the Lay Readers' Association. Together we requested a meeting with the Bishop and some of the more influential Synod officials.

At the ensuing meeting, an effective plan for a ministry at All Saints' was put forward. This expressed the needs of the Sunday congregation present and future, but more especially the great social service needs of the locality. Briefly, the proposal was that All Saints' cease to be a normal parish church and become a church-community centre. The following points were also made: (1) Sunday worship would continue as in the past. (2) A Board of Directors would operate All Saints' with the rector as Director or Chaplain. The Board would consist of parish members, diocesan appointees, interested laymen. Five such interested laymen were ready to serve immediately. (3) A financial budget would be offered. (4) As funds became available, consideration should be given to reducing the size of the church nave to make extra space convenient for meetings and other uses. (5) The plan should be an experiment for two years. After two years' trial period, the diocese would be free to change or discontinue the ministry. This could involve the sale of property.

This plan was generally approved by the Bishop and his advisors. Since the men presenting the plan were men of repute, their offer to be responsible for finance and organization was appreciated. However, in order to change the system and the personnel management, it was necessary that the church be disestablished and cease to be a parish.

(The congregation just did not have members capable of running a church that faced such a challenge in downtown Toronto.) There would henceforth be no wardens, no Advisory Board; other fringe benefits included the very cheering fact that there would be no diocesan apportionment for the church to pay. The rector would cease to be a rector, and become Director, Priest-in-Charge, or What-have-you.

Plans were made for future meetings. The proposal must be brought to the wardens first, then to the vestry meeting of all members of All Saints'. But there was a general feeling of well-being. All Saints' had long been a diocesan headache, keeping bishops awake at night. Now it seemed that a worthwhile solution with a positive aspect had been put forward.

A meeting with the wardens and a planning committee gave approval. Here tremendous help was given us by Bishop Garnsworthy, at that time in charge of urban affairs in the diocese. He had already shown great patience with us in the past. So had our diocesan bishop, George Snell; if he had not been a gentleman as well as a bishop, we would have been out of business by now. The continued patience of these two men has been throughout a great factor in the prosecution of the plan.

Shortly after, the vestry met to consider the matter. There were about forty-odd people present. Opinion was expressed that this was the best proposal we had so far received. Although there was regret over the rather drastic word "disestablishment" (we had our share of anti-disestablishmentarians!), there was general happiness that the ministry of the church would continue, and that the buildings would be preserved – and preserved to some purpose. Only about half a dozen people opposed, so a resolution was sent to the Synod of the diocese stating that the congregation of All Saints' accepted the proposed plan of disestablishment, and placed the property and financial assets of the church in the hands of the Synod to be kept in trust for the ministry. This was a fine thing, really beautiful. For people who themselves, or whose fathers and grand-fathers, had controlled these large buildings, this expensive property, were willing to take a chance and put all they loved so much into the hands of the Synod authorities, with the confident trust that there might be honour among bishops (as among those of an even older occupation) and that their minority rights would be respected. All this demanded quite an act of faith, especially as we were faced with a two-year trial term, and were sitting on a site worth half a million dollars. Would the diocese think that a ministry giving few practical returns, but serving the "bums" of Sherbourne Street, was worth half a million?

March 1, 1971: The new regime officially open-ed. As one of my last official rectorial acts I had, with the wardens, conveyed the property to the diocese – the most expensive gift I have ever made or am ever likely to make! The records were surreptitiously removed to the Synod office by a zealous churchwar-den, leaving the church-safe as bare as Mother Hub-bard's. A sense of freedom descended on us. The first board, meeting a few days earlier, had established themselves; they were ten men and women nomi-nated by us but appointed by the Bishop, and among them were the two former wardens. A chairman was appointed and members were put in charge of various fields of activity – worship, outreach, maintenance, use of church facilities, finance.

I should explain here that this Board is really in an advisory capacity to the minister (or director) and congregation. The area of control is difficult to determine but, considering the high level of friendship and trust, we do not anticipate any conflict of power. As minister (or director), I am regarded as the catalyst of the organization and am constantly in touch with the chairman regarding the initiation of new plans. The Board continually insists that they are resource people to serve the minister and congregation, and that I am largely responsible for the conduct of the church and organization. Because they are almost all members of other congregations, there is little danger of their becoming lay-popes, as is so often the sad tale with church-wardens. The chairmanship and other offices will rotate. While I am reduced or perhaps elevated to the position of director or chaplain, I am the freest clergyman with a "parish" in the diocese. I am in no way controlled by the congregation, for they are all so new, so transient, and many are known only by their Christian names. (There has been, however, a yearly sort of church meeting at which all members of the congregation may express their thoughts.) But since I work with a group of friends who are advisors and resource people, decisions can be made very quickly. In an area where there is little local leadership, or where local leaders may well develop into Frankensteins or demagogues, I think this is an admirable pattern for others to adopt. We ourselves adopted such a policy because it was a necessity: it has now become our very real strength. We suggest that for many other churches, downtown and in rural areas, especially where leadership is scarce, this would be a great improvement. God forbid that, however strong we become in future, we should ever go back to the old system.

With regard to "disestablishment" – in our case no one really knows what it actually means, for the church continues to operate. Primarily, we are no longer a parish, in the sense that the traditional parish setting – e.g., wardens, Board of Management, vestry meetings, parish boundaries – have been abandoned. The Synod apportionment, which every parish pays, is no longer paid by us. It has been suggested that this happy fact is our real reason for wanting disestablishment! But actually in this way our parish has found itself. The "parish that went out of business" (to quote the title given by an Anglican Church House publication to All Saints') has truly become a parish. It is no longer "congregational", as so many Canadian Anglican churches indeed seem to be to an English Canadian. The parish has become the community – not the congregation or organization, but rather the people who live anywhere near. This is the true sense of the ecclesiastical parish; the parish set-up of All Saints' had to be done away with, disestablished, to become a living parish in the right sense of the word.

In this "new" parish, worship is still regarded as vital, and the heart of all that we do, but it is only a part of the total Christian operation. We have – we believe we *must* have – a real concern for any parishioner or community dweller, of any denomination or more likely none, as the one for whom the church primarily exists. This great point was expressed by the Archbishop of Canterbury at the Toronto Worldwide Anglican Congress of 1962, and this is what I understand in the induction charge: "Receive this charge, thy care and mine." Ultimately, this will mean that every Canadian in this Dominion, and every immigrant too, may be under the care and responsibility of the Christian Church through its parishes. '

So now the Christian community gathered in and around All Saints', at the junction of Sherbourne and Dundas streets, was ready for action. Her own house was beginning to be set in order, as much as could be expected in that geographical area of crisis and decay; now we could look outside to action. What would be our ministry? What were our terms of reference for a Christian ministry? Here we had recourse to the scriptures; and for those who will regard us as iconoclasts or modernists or social-gospel-oriented, may I point out that behind the change in form at All Saints', behind the new total ministry, was the solid backing of the documents of the Christian gospel. The whole thing, we maintain, was based on theology, and on the life, experience, and ministry of Christ and His first Christians, on the worship and practice of the primitive Church.

Three great passages of New Testament theology were firmly behind all our thoughts, planning, endeavours. The first was the famous "kenosis" (self-emptying) passage (Phil. 2: 5-9), on the self-giving, self-abandonment of Jesus:

> Let this mind be in you, which was in Christ Jesus: Who, being in the form of God, thought it not robbery (a prize to be snatched at) to be equal with God: But made Himself of no reputa-

tion, and took upon Him the form of a servant, and was made in the likeness of men: And being found in fashion as a man, He humbled Himself and became obedient unto death, even the death of the Cross. Wherefore God also hath highly exalted Him, and given Him a name which is above every name.

We believe that it is necessary that every Christian share something of this experience of Jesus of Nazareth, a self-surrender, something of the Cross, in order to reach the glory of the Resurrection. To say this might be trite and commonplace, but to experience it is not too commonplace. Yet must this not be the experience of every group of Christians, of each Christian cell and, much more so, of the Church, which dares to name herself the Body of Christ? Will she not experience and share a little of the sufferings of that body of Christ?

Following the Depression and the blitz of World War II, I came from England to the prosperous rural and town churches of Canada, where everyone went to the church of his choice. What was so hard for me to comprehend was this, "Where is the Cross in all this?" There seemed so little resemblance to the suffering Church of the New Testament or of the sub-apostolic days. The church was so popular, with church-building a major industry; it just did not seem to be the Church of the New Testament. It was all too easy, too comfortable. But *eheu fugaces anni labuntur* and the scene has changed. Now we may see, at least nearer the city, the various churches and congregations sharing all the different shades of the life and experience of Jesus. There are churches in the smaller towns where the parish life is still suited to the life of a small town. There are also churches in the outer suburbs of the one-house, one-family type where people traditionally do go to church; these churches are full on Sundays, and active through the week too, and are in a way sharing the happy Galilean ministry of Jesus – flowers and sunshine, popularity and large crowds. Come a little nearer to the city; the church is still strong here in the inner suburbs, but problems are beginning to emerge – shadows on the horizon, the first muttering of the storm, like the beginning of the persecution of Jesus. Come into almost downtown, where the churches are sharing the hardships of Jesus; it is a hard uphill struggle like the journey to Jerusalem. And when you get really into the city, the squalid city, you see the churches wrestling like Jesus on trial or in the garden of Gethsemane. When you get right down into the inner city, you witness the churches uttering the cry of dereliction, passing through the Cross of Christ Himself.

Here, it is our greatest glory that there were some who were willing to share this self-abandonment, this self-emptying and laying aside of glory – who were ready to give up their church and their beautiful buildings, which they had learned to love for ages, to the mean and shabby, the drunk, the prostitute, the careless and unwashed, the naturally deprived and self-destroyed remnants of society. This was to share some little of the agony, the self-abasement of Jesus Himself; this was to pass through a little of the Cross. But having done this, having passed through something of the Cross, it is tremendous fun on the other side. We believe we share, in the life of our church, something of the Resurrection and the excitement of Pentecost.

The second great passage that gave us our terms

of reference for a mission in the slums is in the
Gospel of ·Luke (4: 18-19). Here Jesus sets forth
vividly the plan of His ministry. This passage,
occurring as it does in the setting of His home-
town church, probably near the beginning of His
ministry – and in a vital place in the gospel narra-
tive – surely expresses the very essence of His work.
He comes to Nazareth, and stands up to read the
scripture; He is given the book of the prophet
Isaiah, finds a chosen passage and reads:

> The Spirit of the Lord is upon me, because he
> hath anointed me to preach the Gospel to the
> poor; he hath sent me to heal the broken-hearted, to
> preach deliverance to the captives, and recovery of
> sight to the blind, to set at liberty them that are
> bruised. To preach the acceptable year [Year of
> Jubilee] of the Lord. . . .

And when He has the attention of everyone present, He says: *"This day is this scripture fulfilled in
your ears."* He declares that this is His job, His
work; this is why He has come.

Surely, then, a ministry in a poor and deprived
area – a ministry perhaps even more urgently
required than that at Nazareth – is the job for us.
This is the perfect place for the perfect ministry of
Jesus, as put forward in this passage of the Gospel.
Here are our terms of reference, right from the lips
of Jesus. It is clearly spelled out for us by the best
of all men at one of the great moments of His life.

The final scriptural passage that moved us
greatly, and seemed to come alive, was the First
Epistle of Peter, a letter sent under the name of
the apostle to the small, scattered churches of Asia
Minor, the very simple groups of early Christians.
The emphasis of the passage in Peter 1: 9-10 is on

the discovery of community *(koinonia)*, fellowship among the early Christians. We picture the letter being read to a very mixed congregation, of rich and poor, but probably mostly poor, with a few slaves among them, and of very different races, far away from their homes. "You," he writes, "were not a people" – just a collection of individuals from all over the Roman world, Romans, Greeks, Syrians, Jews, perhaps a Negro – "You were not a people, but now are the People of God."

They had been without a home, without a nation, but now they were in the family of God, and citizens of His Kingdom. This fellowship they had found in the Church. We feel something like this, as we look around at our little congregation of about fifty people, a very mixed bag, of very different races and several nationalities, many far from home, many wandering from city to city, and many with no family near by or perhaps no relatives at all. Yet in the fellowship of our little congregation, or in some social activities here, they are beginning to find themselves, to discover community, to find a sense of belonging. And in exalted moments I want to say: "You who were not a people once are now the people of God, a family, a fellowship." For this is what these lonely people, many of them old people, need – a sense of belonging to God and to one another. Isn't this one of the main objectives of the Church today?

CHAPTER V
THE USE OF OUR BUILDINGS

"The nave of the church presents the last religious field for Christianity to conquer." This was the caption beneath a picture of our church as the pews were being moved out.

We had wondered what to do with a huge, rather fine, if slightly colourless nave of a church, which was nearly always empty. For almost a hundred years it had been a holy place, "the dear old church", a place of worship and nothing else. Here was our first and greatest challenge. Our answer to this would express our whole theology of the church and our outlook to the community.

It had long been my dream to make the church buildings, and especially the church itself (the "sanctuary", if you are United Church), into a "People's Place". We had already dared to call it a "Jesus Place". So this would be a place of meeting – a Jesus Place and a People's Place, a place where people might meet Jesus and one another. This was, we believe, already happening in the Parish Hall with the Men's Coffee-House, and also in the Baldwin Hall with the mental health group activities. But what of the vast area of the church itself – it was a very fine building, Victorian, Gothic, and greatly admired by the University School of Historical Architecture, with its rather good stained-glass windows and pews to seat 500 bodies. It had not mattered in the recent past, apparently, that only about ten percent of these pews had at any one time been used in this generation. There they were, and they would remain until the day when the people would come back to church! But obviously now something had to be done about them.

Pews, wooden pews, heavy wooden pews, row after row they stood in their massed defiant ranks in martial array of English oak and brown ecclesiastical uniform, beneath the flags of Empire and Dominion, impervious to change, impervious to cannon-fire. So sure, so stolid, so stable, proclaiming the stability, the rigidity, the iron immovability of Victorian religion and Victorian Sundays, and redolent of that sacred odour that clings to church furnishings. It did not matter that they were the most uncomfortable pews that the Devil or man had so far contrived. This was all part of the glamour of Protestantism! It did not matter that numerous little Protestant and protesting children had fallen backwards through them and hit their Protestant and protesting heads on the hard floor below. It didn't matter that the pews spoiled the architecture of the building, or that, because of the pews, one could do nothing else in the building but sit or kneel or stand. No, there is a form of primeval piety which suggests that pews are good for people and meant – especially in Canada – to hurt people's knees or develop an incipient curvature of the spine. Pews are the essence of Victorian religion – all that is good, all that is bad about it.

So what would we do with a building full of great heavy pews? How from this would we make a People's Place? It was rather like making a bowling green on a battlefield. Quite obviously we had to do some furniture-removing. A start was made surreptiously. About ten pews were moved away, leaving a fair number in the front for public worship. Now we had a gap, a yawning chasm in between, with a vast sea of pews reaching off towards the western horizon into the setting sun, at the back of the church. If I had at any time hoped that people mightn't notice this on the following Sunday, when the act of sacrilege was revealed to the congregation, I was sadly mistaken. The effect was electrifying. I had laid my hands on holy things! I had broken the local taboo. If I had carved my name on the altar or prayed for the dead or expectorated into the lavabo, I couldn't have done worse. The congregation had valiantly endured all sorts of preaching, off-beat stuff from Bishop Robinson and Bonhoeffer; they had suffered criticism of some of their dearest beliefs; they had accepted a cross on the Communion Table. But this final act – this removing of pews, this destroying of the church – this was to attack the very roots of Christianity and all that the Empire stood for.

After the tumult and the shouting had died down, and with the blessing of the new Board and the advisory skill of an architect member of the same Board, a plan was adopted. A worship centre was created in the front of the church; pews were left to seat about eighty people, which with the addition of the choir stalls would provide for up to one hundred people, while all the remaining pews were uprooted. Here at last was an answer to the perennial problem of how to get people to the front of the church – take away the other seats! So our worship space was cosy and snug, tending to give an element of closeness and fellowship which immediately improved the whole feeling of the Sunday worship itself. At the back, a screen of bright-coloured curtains was provided by the ladies of the Diocesan Chancel Guild. This was not so much to divide off holy from unholy ground; still less was it intended to separate the sheep from the goats, for there is a good deal of intermingling on either side of the velvet curtain; but it gave a more compact feeling to our place of worship. Also, to those of us who still had religious hang-ups, it gave a greater sense of freedom when in the rest of the church building, which immediately became a community centre. The pews met various fates; some were sold for irreligious purposes. We had tried to fit them in other parts of the buildings, and even took them out into Dundas Street and stopped the street cars in the attempt, but since they wouldn't bend, there was no door through which we could take them. We painted quite a few bright gold and red, and put these around the walls of the church, matching doors of the same colour. The small pews, originally from the transepts, were quite in demand and helped to close off little offices in the transepts, where presently different groups serve people who come in for various needs.

A good deal of work was done to improve and brighten the interior of the church and to fill up the vacant acreage. Colour was needed, for only religious people can live with dull colours, and we were looking for people who were not religious at all. The vast area of the floor was comprised of dirty grey softwood boards; we partly covered these by rather bright carpets scrounged from the Royal York Hotel. Later the whole floor was sanded and stained a good colour. A gift of black leather couches and chairs was made by the Downtown Church Workers' Associates. Now, it is a good sight to see a group of really poor people gathered around the TV, sitting in executive chairs with their feet on a carpet that once adorned the Royal York, or sitting at gaily draped coffee-tables – such a change from the single cluttered-up room of a rooming-house where so many live and are lonely. We had flowers and plants; we tried to get a fountain and a palm-tree, but so far haven't come up with either. Now the whole building was completely changed, brightened; the architecture was revealed without obstruction. The old, latent dignity of the building was no longer obscured by the pews. All was open, lovely, surrounded by bright stained-glass windows. The dignity, the beauty had in no way been marred or spoilt, but rather enhanced. A barren waste had become a place of colour and joy and laughter, a place where it was nice to be. A place where religion and ordinary life were blended together, and the separations of sacred and profane (in the sense of "common") no longer existed.

The place was now ready for action. Religion would yield to Christianity! Not only would we pray for all sorts and conditions of men, but the doors would in a day or two be flung open to

them. Here would be a place of rest and refresh-
ment for lonely people who otherwise would be
just sitting in their rooms looking at four walls, or
walking the streets, or passing time in the pub. We
would try to provide services for the greatest needs
of the neighbourhood; these services or agencies
would be located in the transepts or side-aisles in
little offices, and – if we could gather such services
in – they would give help in matters of mental
health, unemployment, room-registry, addiction,
legal-aid, care of Canadian Indian children, and
general counselling. The dream was about to be
fulfilled.

And we would find our worship to be more real,
more related to life, because we worked and played
in the same building; we would find, too, that our
work and play were more worthy because we
prayed in the same building. This would be our
discovery – that the best kind of church is not the
sacred shrine or "high place", set aside for Sunday
and nothing else, but rather the place of people
meeting with people and with God, especially in
the common things of life.

CHAPTER VI

THE "OPEN DOOR" TO A SECULAR CHURCH

Outside the newly painted orange doors of our church (with apologies to all who like their religion served up in dull brown) is a notice: THE OPEN DOOR. It should, of course, be taken for granted that a church door will be open – after all, what is the good of a locked-up church? Yet we realize that churches are apt to get wrecked, their buildings misused, their carpets stolen (some churches stamp their carpets every yard with the text "Stolen from St. Mary's" or whatever!). So, when the religious people were in charge of our church, it was kept pretty well under lock and key, and I used to accuse our caretaker of being descended from a long line of jailors at the Bastille. But now, beautifully, the "Open Door" proclaims that we are welcoming people and offering the hand of friendship – at least from ten a.m. to four p.m.!

In the last chapter we spoke of a dream, something perhaps of a vision. It was a vision of what the nave of the church might become, how it might be enjoyed by God's children; a vision of our lovely large building as not only a place of worship

on Sunday, but one of fellowship through the
week, a community centre. Most of the mechanics
had already been performed; now the vision was
about to become a reality.

The vision has also pictured a group of people
from agencies and service groups working in the
side-aisles, ready to help those who came in with
various problems. Meanwhile, folks would be
relaxing with a cup of coffee in a rather less austere
atmosphere than that of a lineup for clothing or
food vouchers, or the tenseness of a medical centre.
We were fortunate to find such service groups for
our building. They have occasionally changed for
various reasons; some have moved to other accom-
modations or because they lost their funding, but
there are or have been such groups as the Canadian Indian Children's program, Legal Aid, an
employment agency, a Maritime service, a mental
health workshop, the Indian Addiction Centre, the
Downtown Community TV, and, in particular con-
junction with the Open Door, the Room Registry
Service. These services have helped provide for
many of the very real needs of our poor transient
population – needs such as living accommodation,
addiction, unemployment, mental instability, problems of law, immigration, and adapting to city life,
as well as the need for companionship and consult-
ation. The Downtown Community TV was perhaps something different; it gave us a good deal of
advertising on the Rogers Cable TV Community
show on a Thursday night, notably at the time of
our Centennial, producing our own church TV presentation. This gave us a good relationship with
the community, and was like having a Want-Ad
office built into our fabric.

Just at the time when we were beginning to move out some of the pews – and getting a few dirty looks for doing so – a lady named (most appropriately) Grace, who had some experience in the field of mental health, brought some of the clients of the Dundas Day Care Centre with her, and offered their services in running a Community Centre and Room Registry Service at the back of our church. This would be an excellent form of rehabilitation for the group, as well as an excellent service to the community. It was exactly what we wanted, where we wanted it, and when we wanted it; it would be an admirable Centennial project. We supported their appeal for a L.I.P. (Local Initiative Program) grant for five workers, and they were successful. The group has since been supported by L.I.P. now for about eighteen months, as well as by Metro and the United Way. At this time, too, we installed new washrooms and a kitchen through the gift of the Atkinson Foundation – all most opportune. I am not by nature one who immediately sees the hand of providence in everything that turns out well, but it did seem as if Someone might be on our side.

So the Open Door began – at first as a Drop-In Centre for women, for whom there were fewer places in the neighbourhood than for men. Since that time, men have been allowed to attend, and in fact outnumber the women, because there are so very many more single men around. We feel that some of the quieter men like to come here as a change from the rather large "Friendship Centre" in our Parish Hall, where there is always a big crowd and not unnaturally a good deal of noise.

Also, some of the men like to bring in their girl-friends and vice versa.

We provide coffee, TV, and cards, with bingo and euchre two afternoons a week. May I add that for bingo the prizes are very small – a can of beans or something of the sort; it is not a money-making affair. (At one time a member of our Board did hairdressing, which was a "first" in our church.) There is a small library, newspapers, an occasional lunch on some special occasion, but generally people like to come and chat with one another and with the workers, to relax, to be friendly. Because of our association with the Mental Health Centre, quite a few former patients and people with mental health problems come to us; occasionally the atmosphere is more that of an out-patients' ward in a mental hospital than a parish church, as "by law established". The leader of the Open Door has reported:

> The Centre is a quiet, comfortable, pleasant haven for people when they are lonely or in need of help with their personal problems. Many of the people who come ... are either mentally, emotionally or physically ill and in need of a place where they may escape from their lonely, shabby, rooms for a few hours. Both men and women come to us for help of various kinds and are given our personal attention. Social workers bring some of their people to us for help, as they themselves do not have enough time to give the kind of attention that we try to give. Therapists have sometimes brought their patients to us so that they will have somewhere to spend their time and to find some companionship.
>
> There is no question that a great number of these people would be drinking or walking the

streets as candidates for trouble, if the Centre is forced to close (through lack of funding) ... We find just as many men as women enjoy the peace, quietness and comfort, which they find in this lovely old church. Many tell us that they want to keep away from where they are tempted to drink, and quite a number have requested our help in getting into Detox Centres.

Our Drop-In people consist mainly of Welfare and Medical Welfare recipients, Disability Pensioners, those on an Old Age Pension and also ex-mental patients. Being able to come here for a few hours a day makes their lives a little less miserable, a little more bearable. Many get quite upset everytime they hear that we might have to close the Centre.

A recent count of attendance found that nearly a hundred people come into the Centre each day from Monday to Friday.

The Room Registry Service, which has since the beginning worked with the Open Door and is an integral part of it (as long as we can find funds for staffing), serves about thirty to forty people weekly. The leader of this group gives the following account:

This service has been of help to hundreds of people in need of accommodation. While about half the people we have served in the past 18 months are employed, we mostly aim to help those who are not physically or financially able to seek accommodation for themselves. Although we started out to serve the Ward 7 area, we have branched out to include a large part of the City of Toronto, but because our staff is not large, we are not able to cover the suburban area. We understand, however, that our service is the largest and most used of any in the city.

We get requests and referrals from Welfare Offices, Hospitals, Addiction Research Centre,

Emergency Housing, and many other Social Agencies, as well as the general public. We handle 30 to 40 persons or families weekly, either in person or by telephone and, although this may not seem too large a number, many who contact us are hard-to-place people such as ex-mental patients, alcoholics, drug users, the physically disabled, as well as deserted mothers with several children on a very limited income. With these unfortunate people it often takes much time and effort to try to locate suitable accommodation for them.

Of our five workers, a field-man goes out each day to find, inspect where possible, and list, available accommodation. These are listed at the office at the end of the day. Our files contain about 70 permanent landlords, plus about 400 rooms, flats, apartments, etc. from private landlords. These necessitate being checked constantly to be kept up to date. We have been repeatedly told, by many Social Agencies and people, that this service has been very helpful to them.

Perhaps we should introduce you to some of our clients at the Open Door, some whom we have met in friendship. The workers will never forget their first visitor. The doors of the church burst open, and a woman staggered in wearing a housecoat, with her face dripping blood, her feet bare. She was actually suffering from terminal cancer and in much pain following an operation. They were able to find her a coat, and another room to live in, for her apartment was not much larger than a good-sized cupboard, and she had only a mattress, not a proper bed. They assisted her to move, carrying all her worldly possessions in three bags. This woman became a regular visitor to the Drop-In. It was the only place she could come to for companionship, and help. She credited the

Open Door with saving her life. The last time she came to us she was very ill; when she passed out from the pain, the workers called an ambulance, she died two or three days later in hospital.

On another occasion, a young couple came in to the church, recently from British Honduras and not yet having landed-immigrant status. They were overwhelmed by the big city after their own small country, and seeking to get themselves organized. The Room Registry found them rooms, where I know they have been happy for quite a time. Our law student took up the matter of immigration. A Jamaican whom we knew was able to offer the wife a small job. We gave them our friendship, and felt that we had performed something of a Christian ministry.

We got to know Emily through one of our workers who had previously started an Alcoholics Anonymous group at All Saints'. Emily phoned for help from the A.A. and David had gone to visit her. She appeared to be a "hopeless drunk". David invited her to the Open Door for friendship and recreation, she came for a week and then disappeared. ("Disappeared" – the word often has sinister meaning in our area. It happens so much with our friends; one day they are there, the next day they are missing – in hospital, on a "binge", in jail, perhaps worse.) On a second visit David found Emily lying passed out on the stairs at the top of the fourth floor of her rooming-house. He carried her up and put her on the bed. The room, he says, was in an awful state, infested with cockroaches and mites. Later Emily confided that, if she did not drink, none of the other roomers would speak to her or even give her a cigarette. Through the

Room Registry a better accommodation was found for her. She has since completely changed. She is now well-dressed, happy and bright, has acquired a colour TV, and once a week drops in to see us.

We are also happy about Luigi. A call came to us from the Bathurst Information Centre; could we find a room for an Italian worker who had undergone an unsuccessful operation and was no longer able to work? He was on a disability pension, feeling useless and depressed. He could only afford a low-rent room ($65 a month), and because of his illness needed a private bathroom. We felt it a "little miracle" when almost immediately after receiving this call a new landlady (not known to us before), who possessed a big old rooming-house, offered a basement apartment of three rooms and a private bathroom for rent cheaply to anyone who could do a little light work. The situation was clinched: a social worker took Luigi to the apartment, and our coffee tasted so much sweeter that day.

Hazel, who works devotedly at the Open Door, told of a woman who phoned the Room Registry in desperate need: "She and her four children were leaving her husband that very day. He beat her and she had to find a place immediately. We talked a landlord into taking them into a three-room flat. It wasn't really big enough, but it was the best that we could do.

"But this woman was luckier than some," Hazel continued, and then spoke of a woman on Mother's Allowance, who had been looking for several months for a place for herself and her five children. The most she could afford was $100 a month. Four of her children were at the Children's Aid and would not be returned until she could find suitable accommodation. This was in Toronto, Queen of the Cities, and I mean Toronto of the twentieth century; I have not unconsciously reverted to the back alleys of Dickens' London.

The story of George is quite perplexing. He is 73 and his wife is 83, deaf, partially blind, in a wheel-chair. They live with their two adult sons, who are severely retarded and not allowed out of the house, while a third son is alcoholic. Perhaps not surprisingly, they are being evicted from Ontario Housing. A concerned social worker, of whom there are many in the city, brought George to us after calling nearly all the agencies, officials, and municipal authorities. George has come several times to the Centre; though he cannot read, he likes someone to read his letters and the newspapers to him. What do we do about housing here? Presently George is awaiting the Court Order for eviction, and will then be placed in the City Emergency Housing. This is the kind of situation that makes everybody say, "We can't do anything," and immediately try to pass it on to another agency. We don't know what else people like George can do; at least it is flattering that they come to us as a last resort.

Not all our clients live so dramatic a life. A typical one is Jane. Her child is at the Children's Aid and her husband is in a Salvation Army sheltered workshop, but he does not like her to go out too much. However, she is able to come twice a week – her only outings – for cards and bingo. She likes to come here to talk to people. She calls this place a Home from Home.

Another regular visitor is Mike, very quiet,

unexciting. He is a little retiring, almost childlike, big, strong, gentle. He comes from a farm north of Kingston, where as the only boy he was spoiled by a number of sisters. He speaks affectionately of how his mother would gather her children around her and say family prayers. Here on skid row, he remembers the deep apple pies she used to make on the old farm homestead. He worked for some years as a truck driver until he suffered an injury. He has since made almost a hobby of seeking compensation, going to lawyers and putting the case before them. We don't know if it is wise to tell him to forget it, or if this would take away his main interest in life. Mike is typical of so many men who are really at home in the country and who love the country, but drift inevitably to the city, and to the agencies and facilities which the city provides. Mike is a gentle man, a regular church attender, but he should really be back home.

Bill is an old friend. I have known him since the days when we ran our own coffee-house, some years ago. A veteran with alcoholic tendencies and often not too capable, he was a member of All Saints' Men's Club for some time. He even came to church a few times, but probably against his better principles, and he obviously felt the need to brace himself for the occasion. The last time he came to a church service, he nearly started our first dialogue sermon. I was speaking movingly about the church reaching out to people, when Bill – give him credit for listening – was heard to respond in a loud and audible voice, "They'll never reach me." Then, after the ripple of mirth which succeeded his response, he told us to carry on. Bill has quietened a lot lately; a stroke affected his speech and left hand, and he has had one or two bad spells and a few times in hospital. He used to come and sit in our reception office, which usually looks like the village-store and only lacks a barber's chair to complete the picture. This was a change from Bill's depressing basement room. Then he got started boiling water for coffee for the Open Door, and now has taken this on as a volunteer, and looks after the whole coffee operation. Here he has found something to do, a slight feeling of responsibility, of doing something useful, and has become very happy. As his pastor and his friend, I am most grateful for what the Open Door has done for him.

Mary is an Objibwa. She has visited the Open Door and is happy to have company, someone to talk to and play cards with. Her problem is alcohol, which has separated her temporarily from her two little boys; one is with the Children's Aid, another with friends. Her social worker is very glad the Open Door gives her a place to go to and encouragement against drinking, with the hope that she will get her children back.

These are some of the visitors who have become our friends and made friends with one another. They are of mixed backgrounds and mixed races, and almost none from Toronto itself. Some are very pleasant, friendly, outgoing. Some are troublesome. One or two can disturb the whole show. Some occasionally walk about the building in a state of tension, like lost souls. Others sleep; they may be intoxicated or have spent all night out of doors. Some are epileptic. Some become hysterical and will go out of the church doors screaming. But these are our people, our parishioners whom God has given us to look after. Sometimes I hear that some of the suburban clergy are not quite sure what their ministry really is. We are fortunate. We have only to open the door: someone falls in and we have our ministry for the day.

CHAPTER VII

THE SECULAR CHURCH – APOLOGIA AND MESSAGE

The press, religious periodicals, even television took notice of the unusual changes in All Saints'. Most of the coverage was kindly and intelligent, even appreciative. An eight-minute presentation on the C.B.C.'s "Weekday" program in the summer of 1972 was most encouraging; the interview was well-conducted by Penny Berton and sympathetically introduced by Ken Cavanagh, and we gave the Anglican Church thousands of dollars' worth of free publicity. We were in the headlines, after being unnoticed for forty years! But the special interest of the press is naturally in the bizarre and unusual, and in 1971-2 it was still unusual for a church to turn out the pews and replace them with café tables where people might come in, drink coffee, play cards. One of two large pictures in a Saturday paper showed a couple at one of the tables with playing-cards in their hands, while in the distance was the east end of the church. Another very colourful report on the Open Door quoted a visitor as at first being surprised to see this, but then giving an opinion that it was "after all a good thing".

Now, I am not presently interested in whether cards are wicked or not (they are probably one of the great inventions of mankind). When I see a group of people, many of them with childlike minds, playing cards or bingo in the community centre at the back of our church nave, for no more prize than a can of beans, this to me is no worse than a little child winning a lollipop at a game of Parcheesi or Snakes and Ladders. What I am immediately concerned with is whether the whole thing, of which this is a particular part, is right in a church. I am concerned with the theology behind it all, with such questions as: What is a church for? What should a church be? Where in the world is the Church? Is a church a holy place? Is it a house of God, and who said so? Does He need one? What does "holiness" mean? What is the difference between Christianity and religion? Are they the same?

The above example, the matter of the cards, is a kind of bizarre point intended to get us rolling on the way. Actually, we feel there is very little need for any defence of what we have tried to do in the nave of our church. Most people, even High Church clergy and an occasional Roman Catholic priest or nun, have expressed great happiness and appreciation. The average Anglican seems very happy, and the rather good-natured agnostic really thinks it "beautiful"; I feel I can talk to them very easily about Christianity and what the church is for. We have also received favourable comments from our bishops, one of whom was a member of the choir in the church's palmy days. They have attended lunches in our church, addressing the groups working there, and compared the pattern with that of the great churches of the Middle Ages, where people assembled for drama and for many of the social occasions of the community.

But I want to present this apologia in order to carry the attack into the enemy camp (if there is one). While this is in part an apology, it is also written as a message; the message is that there are perhaps some other churches that might do the same thing!

The Church in the World

What is the Church? And where in the world is the Church?

I will attempt one or two simple answers, backed up by a few writers of rather naughty theological works, writers who have greatly influenced our thinking and moved us in these directions. I have not their theological acumen, but I *can* say that we have in effect done some of the things they have said the Church ought to be doing, and some of these things we have found to work to the glory of God.

In answering the question "What is the Church?", Malcolm Boyd writes:

> Let the Church be itself – not denominational ghettoes with historical excuses, not private clubs with local membership qualifications based on race or economics, not costumed dispensers of would-be "magic", not playing games with God for an hour a week, not a labyrinth of man-made legalisms, not an organizational structure which must remain unquestioned – but *itself*, which means a community of servanthood in the midst of the world's concerns.[1]

[1] Malcolm Boyd, *The Underground Church* (New York: Sheed and Ward, 1968), p. 4.

This would be perhaps a hard criticism of many very worthy, hard-working groups of Christians; but it is not an altogether untrue criticism of so many churches that have in fact become holy clubs.

This theme is also expressed by Bishop Robinson in *The New Reformation*, which presents the image of the church as

> an archaic and well-protected institution for the preservation of something that is irrelevant and incredible. . . . It has characteristics of the dinosaur and the battleship. It is saddled with a plant and program beyond its means, so that it is absorbed with problems of supply and pre-occupied with survival.[2]

How true of the case in hand! In another book, *Why the Sea is Boiling Hot*, he says that "The last thing the Church exists to be is an organization for the religious. Its charter is to be the servant of the world."[3]

A third writer, Colin Williams, states:

> The present structures of the church are so dominated by the church's surrender to its own wordly security, and the church is so imprisoned within the expensive façades of buildings that relate to men only in a limited portion of their life, that she can find renewal only as she surrenders these securities and gets herself out into the world, careless of her own safety or wealth, allowing the forms of her renewed life to grow around all the shapes of wordly need. If the present patterns of congregational life are inadequate to reach out to the drastically altered shape of modern need, then

---

[2] John A. T. Robinson, *The New Reformation* (London: S.C.M. Press, 1960), p. 20.

[3] John A. T. Robinson in *Why the Sea Is Boiling Hot*, a Symposium on the Church and the World (Toronto: Ryerson Press, 1965), p. 30. As quoted by Joan Hollobon, Chapter V 'Digging the Lingo'.

it is idolatry (worshipping a thing for its own sake) to continue a thought-habit which leads us to see the church from the center of a particular structure – local church, building, congregational worship, committees – and which do not give the freedom to see the church as the love of Christ taking form in the world in response to the call of wordly need.[4]

This was the type of reading in which I soaked myself, as I lived hemmed in by buildings which were ill-used and usually a matter of worry, wrestling with ecclesiastical problems that were not really important to my particular ministry, visiting a group of parishioners who were right out of this world (or certainly the world of the inner city), and indulging in a Sunday worship which was dominated by an older group that had become alien to the local neighbourhood. Renewal was not enough (nor is any appeal for "renewal" enough, considering the recent state of the church today's world). The existing structure did not need to be revived: it needed rather to be laid to rest. It had served its time, and had up to a point done well in that time. But now the whole structure was inadequate where it was; the physical and the spiritual structure was geographically and historically an anachronism. To hope to attract poor people here was like trying to teach Americans to play cricket, or like selling peanuts at a funeral. The present structure of the church was really not related to this world, in this century, so the world was having to get along without her.

---

[4] Colin W. Williams, *Where in the World?: Changing Forms of the Church's Witness* (New York: National Council of Churches of Christ in the U.S.A., 1962), p. 59.

Not a renewal but a reformation was necessary for the Church of All Saints'. And it was entirely because we were ready (and able by disestablishment) to bury the past, to forget the institution, to gamble with the matter of our preservation, and begin something that was really different, that we found new life and an exciting future. For a glorious moment we forget what we had in buildings and people *in* the church: we looked at the need around us, and with this picture clearly before us we created a new thing. Our church did take form "in response to the call of wordly need". As Colin Williams asks:

> Does the church stand today, as is often supposed, on the Easter-side of the Cross? Or... does the church stand today before the Cross? Is its mission then to die?... Only as the church dies may it be born again, and thus only will the Word of God become sacramental in the life of the church for the world of our time.[5]

This we humbly believe to have been the experience of our church, a church that through the leading of God's Spirit after previous failure had to die, and so pass through the Cross to the renewed fellowship of Easter Day. We want to proclaim that, after passing through the Cross in this little way, there is all sorts of excitement on the other side. This is the message we would like to tell.

The Church, we claim, is not buildings or the institution but people, and will be where people are, where people live, where they spend their

---

[5] Ibid., p. 58. Williams here quotes C. Ebb Munden III, in "Motive", Jan. 1963, reviewing a series of papers by the Methodist Student Movement.

time, work and play – at the place of meeting. For Jesus was so obviously in the world. I look at His ministry as one of friendship, a coming to seek out friends among the despised people of the day, sinners, prostitutes, tax collectors. These He came to look for, to find as friends and, having made friends with them, to save by restoring to their true and better selves. This friendship – or love – He showered on the widow, the orphan, the friendless, and indeed on anyone who would accept it, through all His life; even in almost His last words on the Cross He addressed Himself to a fellow-sufferer and, in the eyes of the law, a fellow-criminal. This ministry of friendship He fulfilled to the utmost in His death, and in His return again to His friends in the Holy Spirit. We believe the eternal Spirit of Christ is still pursuing this ministry of friendship; here is God in the twentieth century. In the pleading eyes of a bombed-out family, of a starving child, or of an alcoholic to whose better self and innate will-power we are trying to appeal, here is the Christ "incognito". In Bishop Robinson's words:

> If men are to see Christ, and therefore God, they can only do it, through the One who comes to them, in the first instance, not as a Messianic figure, but as one of themselves, as Fred or Harry or the man across the street.[6]

Or, as Rex Dolan says:

> We must enable Christ to walk "incognito" through our involvement in the practical, often material, everyday needs of people. Thus much

---

[6] John A. T. Robinson, *The New Reformation*, p. 35.

> personal evangelism today will likely not include
> "religion" or even invitations to church. . . . Since
> many will be confused and perhaps repulsed by
> "God-talk" and "Jesus-talk", evangelism will
> take place through God's influence as loving
> human concern.[7]

So the Church, which is the people of Christ, must
be where people are, "humbly sharing in His ser-
vanthood in the midst of the secular world" (in
Starbuck's words).[8] This means the Church in the
world, a secular Church.

How often in moments of depression and
nigh-despair I had wondered if I should move my
ministry to the rarified atmosphere of the suburbs,
where people go to church. But this would be to
share the retreat, the strategic withdrawal. If the
church is of no use in the slums, what real use is it
anywhere? What sort of a church is it that only
applies to the affluent? Should I go to the Indian
reserve, then perhaps send resources out there and
teach the children of the reserve to sing "Jesus
loves the Indian boy"? But my own parish was full
of Canadian Indians, some very active and some
who had sunk to the level of the Anglo-Saxon
drop-out. Should I go to the mission-field, to
Africa or India, because the people of Cabbagetown were too tough to convert? No, here I was
on skid row, that station where it had pleased God
to call me, and Christ – the Incognito Christ – was on

---

[7] Rex Dolan, *The Big Change* (United Church of Canada, Toronto
1967), p. 67.

[8] Robert B. Starbuck, in his introduction to Horst Symanowski's *The
Christian Witness in an Industrial Society*, translated by George H.
Kehm (Philadelphia: Westminster Press, 1964), p. 26.

skid row. I had been sent here, and would stay where He was, and where perhaps – greatest of all honours – He needed me most.

Dr. McLeod of the noted Iona Community compares the function of the church to that of salt:

> The purpose of salt is neither to turn everything it touches into salt, nor to remain safely in the jar. Salt reveals and fulfils its saltness only when it releases the full flavour of that into which it has been scattered. The church, in this view, is not an end in itself: it is an instrument of God's love for the world ... The church is in the world to be light, salt for the world's own sake.

Rex Dolan, who quotes this comparison, explains that the church has persistently gone about this function in the wrong way. Either it has tried to "leave the salt in the jar" (that is, keep its activity within the church walls) or "turn the whole world into salt" (try to bring everyone into the particular church community). But in neither case has the church been doing what it is the true function of salt to do. It has been too anxious to protect its own saltness, and so has "failed to bring out the true flavour of life in the world." But the church only becomes salt when it ceases to care about preserving itself, and is ready to "fling itself out into the world as salt is flung into food."[9]

Now surely all of this is to rediscover the Incarnation, which is perhaps the greatest "find" of the Christian Church in recent years – to rediscover Christ in life, in the world, in all humanity, and in all the interests and affairs of humanity – to rediscover in the Incarnation the glory of the common-

---

[9] Rex Dolan, *The Big Change*, p. 26.

place. If we wished in any way to rename our church, it would be as the "Church of the Incarnation", for it is in God's world, where man is, that the Church must be. And sometimes we will meet Christ in the height of man's glory; but sometimes we must dig pretty deep into the depths of humanity, to find Christ there.

The Secular Church and Secular Christianity

This church we have been discussing may well be called the "secular church". We are not referring to the church in any worldly sense, as "being conformed to the likeness of this world"; we mean a church which is in truth missionary, dedicated to serve God's world. There will be in the secular church no idea of saving oneself, or one's little company of like-minded people, out of a perishing world; but rather, if need be, perishing with it for the sake of the world.

For this is what Jesus did, and it may give us a hint to the meaning of the cry of dereliction – "My God, why?" This would be in accord with Abraham's plea for the condemned cities: "peradventure there be found ten righteous men . . . " There is here no thought that these righteous shall be saved out of the city of condemnation, to behold, like so many elect, the evil in the throes of their just torment! No, if the city is to be destroyed, the righteous will suffer with it. If it is to be saved, the righteous will be saved with it. Their salvation is *with*, not *apart from*, the community. So will be the calling of the Church of Christ. We would emphasize that the meaning of the classic text "God so loved the world . . . " is not that God would save some righteous few out of it, but that God would in fact save the world. I believe that the fate of the Church, as the Body of Christ, will be to share the fate of the world. This is an utter rejection of the idea of the "holy club", and of all those creeds, such as Jehovah Witnesses, that look at the world or society as a doomed ship from which to pick up a few survivors. If Jesus is the captain of our ship, He would, if called upon, like a good captain go down with her.

The secular church will make no attempt to flee the world or put itself on a rock above the storm, to run to the monastery, look at life from an ivory castle, or seek refuge and pre-occupation in the usual gamut of church activities, for this would be to leave Christ alone suffering in the world. The church will not seek to lock itself in buildings, for this would be to lock man, and Christ with him, on the outside. Still less will the church seek to preserve her own safety, and the security of her position or vested interests, for these are of no value unless they are in the world. The secular church will not preserve herself within the armour of her creeds, which seems to be a particular hobby of the Anglican Church. Any attempt to look down upon the world or to address it with the voice of authority will not only be ignored, but will be completely out of place, for in the realm of Christianity the only authority is that of Love – in which authority the institutional church has not always earned a very high rating.

The church is in the world *for* the world, for man and God, to bring them together. This was

the purpose of the Incarnation and the whole ministry of Jesus.

Holiness – Christian or Pagan?

The attempt of All Saints', in turning the nave of
the church in part into a community centre, was
one aspect of the secular church. Not many would
quarrel with the idea of welcoming more sinners
than saints into church, even into a church dedicated as "All Saints' ". What may be harder to
defend is what might be called the de-sacralization
of things which have always been regarded as
sacred. We have been taught since childhood that
there are certain holy things, holy places, holy
days, even holy people. Most of us, unless we are
very rabid Protestants, have some such feeling
about our churches and our sanctuaries (so do
many people who do not go to church). Is this a
virtue or a hang-over?

For example, I have been taught to acknowledge
the Cross on the Communion Table with rever-
ence: now, at a Festival of Faith in full glory of
bishops, canons, and choirs, I see teenagers sitting
in the sanctuary (because there is nowhere else for
them to sit), laughing and talking, all in an act of
worship. I have been used to blasting children for
running around in the church, and telling them not
to shout and so on. Now I see people playing
cards at the back of the church, and find myself
even rolling a cigarette. Then I ask myself: When I
acknowledge the Cross, when I bow my head to
the Cross, what am I doing? Am I prostrating

myself before an awful deity who will smite me
with boils if I do not? Or if I neglect some word of
deference, fail to spell God with a capital "G", or
in my worship omit some word of ritual, the holy
incantation, will my prayers not be heard? I
answer, "No." This Cross stands for a God of
Love: it is Love in the Name of Jesus, Who is the
personification of Love, Whom I worship. The
Cross stands not for fear, but for Love. I may be
afraid in many places, but not in the church. Let
the children be happy here; who am I to forbid
them? Let God's people be happy and play like
children, for so many really are children. For all
that is lovely and happy and decent is dear to the
heart of God.

So what about this word "*holy*"? Is it a part of
the Christian or the pagan heritage? Is it a vital
part of the teaching of Christ and His first followers, or is it a later accretion from the paganism of
Greece, Hebraism, and the mystery-religions,
Mithraism, and so on? Christ produced this wonderful thing called Christianity, a faith, a movement, which was first known in apostolic days as
"The Way" (Acts 9:2). He brought God and love
into the ways and places of men, the fields, the
streets, the homes. The early Christians met for
simple remembrance of Jesus in one another's
homes; they emphasized fellowship, the breaking of
the bread, eating their meat with gladness and
singleness of heart (Acts 2:46). They emphasized
joy and happiness. But a few decades later they
had begun to put His open way of life back again
into buildings and shrines; they built churches, or
what would come to be churches, walled off and

sanctified Christianity, made it one more religion, made the breaking of the bread a religious ritual, separated the Eucharist from the Agape. They revived the old sense of "taboo", built again the sacred shrine or holy ground marked off for the god, and eventually erected magnificent cathedrals rivalling the Temple of Solomon, although even Solomon apologized for presuming to think that God would dwell in a Temple made by hands (I Kings 8:27). As Leslie Weatherhead in *The Christian Agnostic* has written:

> Many wonder how the elaborate ritual and ceremony of some services can possibly have developed from the teaching of a young man in a boat on the Sea of Galilee, Who talked so simply and yet so profoundly and relevantly to very simple people.[10]

This idea is reinforced by Louis Evely, a noted Roman Catholic theologian who has recently left the official priesthood, in his book *If the Church Is to Survive*. He writes:

> Christ systematically desacralized everything that, in his time, was considered sacred. He desacralized the Temple: "Destroy this Temple . . ." He said. "You will worship the Father neither on this mountain nor in Jerusalem." He desacralized the priests and he preferred heretics who served their brothers to them. He desacralized ascetic practices, the fine distinctions between "pure" and "impure", and religious fasts, by describing them all as old wine-skins. He desacralized worship by telling his followers that before they worshipped they must first go and be reconciled with their

---

[10] Leslie D. Weatherhead, *The Christian Agnostic* (Abingdon Press, 1965), pp. 113-14.

brothers, and by insisting that mercy was more important than sacrifice. He even desacralized the sabbath, the sacred day par excellence instituted and respected by God Himself. "The sabbath was made for man, and not man for the sabbath."

He taught that the only things really sacred were those that were most ordinary and most profane: man, the laity, the people, the poor . . .

. . . It was a scandal, and one which was visited upon the early Christians by those most religious men who despised and taunted them by asking, "What is this new sect? Where are your temples, where are your priests, where are your sacrifices? There is nothing religious to you. You are atheists." And the Christians answered proudly, "Yes, we are atheists so far as your false gods are concerned, your gods are hidden away in your temples, served by our priests, and nourished by your sacrifices. We are all priests, and we offer to God the spiritual sacrifices of our whole lives. We are the true temple of our God, who does not live among stones but in the hearts of men. We break and share bread in our homes, in joy and simplicity, so that they are no poor among us."

And yet two centuries later, under Judeo-pagan influence, the Christians had adopted everything that they had rejected earlier. They began building sumptuous temples that they dared to call "houses of God". They multiplied the "sacred orders". They organized solemn and mysterious liturgies which, they thought, placed them in communication with God. And they stopped sharing among themselves. The old God, the Boss, the Omnipotent egocentric, had regained his place – and naturally the poor man had regained his....[11]

But all this is by no means negative. There is here no intentional shocking of old ladies with

[11] Louis Evely, *If the Church Is to Survive* (Doubleday, 1972), pp. 82-5.

iconoclastic remarks. If we lose a little sense of the "holy", it is only that we may find a newer freedom. I would say this of the Incarnation, for instance; by removing a little of its so-called holiness, we come to see its true meaning. To me, the narratives of the birth of Jesus – the Virgin Birth, still less the Immaculate Conception – in no way heighten the wonder of the Incarnation, but rather are in danger of reducing it to the level of pagan literature. They have significance, but also serve to present Jesus as yet another of the unnaturally born heroes and demi-gods which abound in the religious myths of so many faiths. *This* is not the marvel of the Incarnation. There is nothing that is bizarre or exotic about the Christian Incarnation. It is not "holy", but instead "un-holy", in the sense that it is natural. The wonder of the whole wonderful event is that the Divine is invading the secular, the common, the natural, human history and human life; or perhaps that He really belongs there. And that as He does this in the birth of Jesus of Nazareth, so will He enter all life. The common and the sacred are become one. The Incarnation is not merely God in flesh once: it is God in all life.

Thus, while religion separates the sacred from the profane (because all the gear of religion must be sacred and holy), Christianity joins the two together again, or rather admits of no such separation. There is no such thing as holy ground or consecrated earth, for all God's world is sacred; we cannot by ritualistic acts make it other, for no longer do we look at nature as fearsome in essence, or as deliberately opposed to man. There is no such thing as a holy man, for all the believers are now the priesthood (I Peter 2:9). There is no such thing as a holy place, for any place may be sacred where God is honoured and mankind is served.

Something like this was behind all our thinking of the rearrangement of the nave of All Saints' Church. The sanctuary, the chancel and the front of the nave are as like a good church as any can be – open, wide and beautiful – and receive respect from all but the more unusual characters. This space is our "church". The rest is the "community centre". It might have been separated off by some insuperable barrier; it might have been completely enclosed. But no: we wanted the "churchy" part open to the community, and the community part open to the "religious" (forgive these terms) so that here the sacred and the secular would meet together under one roof, and one God. We resisted at our Board a proposal to screen off the offices in the transepts (although we had already bought the lumber), for we liked the openness, and we wanted people to see all the good things that were going on for God's glory and His people – for God's glory could *be* people. We wanted to feel that what goes on in the worship-centre helps all that goes on in the community centre, and all that goes on in the community centre is the result of what happens in the worship centre; that the worship of God and the fellowship of man are not too far apart, or on different days or in different places. We wanted this to be a sign that the sacred and the secular are together; that there is in fact one God of Love, a Christian God, for the religious and for the non-religious; that, whether we are singing the "Te

Deum" or talking to a drunk, we are equally serving God in the way of Christ; that we in fact do not know where the sacred and the secular begin or end, but we do know they have a common meeting-place in Christ. And this is what the Incarnation is all about.

Religion and/or Christianity

We have anticipated this final theme by our talk of the "holy" or the sacred and the profane. A few more remarks may be relevant to my expression earlier that the nave of our church was "the last religious field for Christianity to conquer".

A text which I tell my sons can be worked into nearly all examinations in the realm of Arts is found in the *De Rerum Natura* of Lucretius, a Latin poet, philosopher and scientist of the late first century: *Tantum religio potuit suadere malorum*. This means, roughly, "So much harm could religion persuade men to do." Lucretius wrote with reference to the sacrifice of the beautiful maiden Iphigenia; how much more might he have written if he had heard of the Crusades, lived through the Thirty Years' War, endured the fires of Smithfield or the Spanish Inquisition or the "religious" wars of Ireland ... The tale of horror in the name of religion is too terrible to utter.

When I think of religion and religious things, I suppose I should say "religiosity" or "churchianity", but I will stick to the word "religion" in the poorer sense of the word. When I speak of religion, then, I think of Synods and Conferences, Rules and Creeds, Sabbaths and Victorian hymns (especially those written for children by the wives and sisters of country clergy), Canvasses and Campaigns, Mrs. Pardiggle and Mrs. Jellyby, tracts like the "Washerwoman of Clapham Common", school prayers and compulsory church parades, crosses, candles and chasubles, funeral homes and canned music, organs with vibrato stop fully unleashed, Bible punchers and Holy Rollers and a good bit of the Hebrew scriptures. The list could go on forever, including all the un-nice things associated with religion, and unfortunately all the un-nice people we meet going round in circles in religious circles, such as clergy going after livings and their wives going after wives of other clergy.

When I think of Christianity, on the other hand, I think of Christ and doing good, and all the fine people I have met in and out of churches who were Christians. I think of all that is lovely in creation, in man, in churches too. I think of the open air and the mountains and beauty, but also I think of the drunks on Sherbourne Street, our friends among them, and the ones we may by the grace of God have been able to help, and whose friendship we have valued.

What have we done with Christianity? How have we managed to make so lovely a thing as Christianity into so horrible a religion? I see a picture in one of Dickens' novels: Little Dorrit and her retarded friend are playing on the step of the house by the street, and across the road is the Parish Church, cold and bare, and bleak as only a Victorian church can look in the rain, fog, and smoke in industrial England. But the whole church is dark, closed up. The place which should have had its doors open, wide open to the local people – the place that should have been a place of love and warmth and light – is bolted and shut like a jail. The place that should have been so kind and welcoming to these children is there, just across the street, but no good. This was a religious building, but at that particular time it was not a Christian building. To me, thinking of that picture, it became a symbol of so many religious buildings; it might have been a factory or a warehouse; there was nothing of God about it. It couldn't have been a house of God, because it was shut and unloving. And this is religion without Christianity, or to give another turn to a popular phrase, "Christianless Religion".

Bishop Robinson blames the church for stripping Christ of His "incognito", and presenting Him to men as the Son of God, rather than allowing them to meet Him first as the Son of Man. The church, he says, has offered Christ as a set figure in creed and doctrine, telling men to meet Him there; whereas the first disciples had to meet Jesus, both before and after His Resurrection, first as a man, and only later find that He was Son of God. Robinson believes that modern men will most likely meet Him "in the way", where they are, as the "gracious neighbour" rather than as the "gracious God".[12]

Louis Evely asks whether Jesus ever meant to found a religion, still less an institution with hierarchy, rites and laws: "Or did He order His disciples to preach the good news?"[13] And this good

---

[12] John A. T. Robinson, *The New Reformation*, p. 35.
[13] Louis Evely, *If the Church Is to Survive*, p. 79.

news would abolish castes, intermediaries between God and man (as Himself the supreme High-Priest); it would announce no other law but that of love; it would remove any gulf between priest and layman, between scholar and simple man, between rich and poor, between man and woman, between sacred and profane; and it would proclaim a God who wished to be worshipped not so much in elaborate form by "specialized priests" but rather in spirit and in truth everywhere and for ever. Finally, Evely writes:

> As paradoxical as it may seem, a religion which centers on God in order to praise Him, appease Him and ask Him favours, is a purely human religion. Christianity, on the other hand, is divine because it reveals a God who is not made in our image: a God who is a gift, love, the pouring out and diffusion of himself, a God whom man is incapable of inventing.[14]

The church-community of All Saints' finds that its ministry cannot be better expressed than in such words as these. We find strength from the writers we have quoted. This is the open form of ministry – Christianity, we hope – which we have adopted especially in the Open Door and in the fellowship-worship of what we call the Agape Supper, in which a new church and congregation has been created according to the pattern of the fellowship-meal of the early Christians, involving a group of families and individuals who, without wishing to be religious, are concerned with the love of God and one's neighbour.

---

[14] Ibid., p. 9.

CHAPTER VIII

"TO PROCLAIM THE GOSPEL TO THE POOR"

Be assured, all ye who at this point may be apt to speak disparagingly of what you may call "just the social gospel" – we *do* proclaim the gospel. (And let us remember that the biblical word is "proclaim", not "preach", which is a bad translation, with due respect to King James and all his works. The original Greek word means heralding, proclaiming.) But on this matter I am unable to separate the gospel of speaking from the gospel of doing. I don't believe that Jesus could, or that He tried to do so. Jesus spent as much time doing the gospel as He did speaking it – one is simply the complement of the other. Speaking proclaims why we do something, and doing assures the sincerity of what we say. We also have to remember that in a depressed area, where for generations people have felt alienated from society and from the church, and have come to distrust all institutions from the jail to the street-corner mission, it will take years of doing the gospel before they will listen to the gospel. They must see love, before they will hear of it; they must find the brotherhood of man before they will accept the fatherhood of God. ("For he that loveth not his brother whom he hath seen, how can he love God Whom he hath not seen?" I John 4:20.)

But we do also try to *proclaim* the gospel to the poor. When we say the "poor", I suppose we cannot be sure whether Jesus meant spiritually or economically poor. I think, however, that the quotation from Isaiah refers to those distressingly poor, and that the Magnificat – "He hath filled the hungry with good things and the rich He hath sent empty away" – is fairly convincing proof that Jesus is definitely concerned with those who do not have enough to eat or enough of this world's goods to live a full life. I feel, too, that when Jesus condemns the wealthy, even the righteous wealthy, He is telling them that their excess of possessions may be actually depriving other people of a fair allowance: this may be why it is hard for a rich man to enter the Kingdom. I have also a lurking fear that when He tells the rich young ruler to sell all he has and give it to the poor, He is telling all would-be disciples to do this very thing. Christendom has failed, I think, largely because it never widely presented any really Christ-like approach to the problem of wealth and power; we have failed because the gospel was never really applied to the economic system. The church has usually shown extraordinary ability to adapt to the society in which she has found herself, even to the extent of fashioning the law of love into a system of gain, and the law of "give" into a system of "get". It is very hard to be a true Christian in present-day society.

So we proclaim the gospel to the poor. It is the

gospel of friendship, friendship which means love, and love which is the Christian name for God. It was Jesus who gave God this name. And anything in religion or in the church or in the Bible, any action, any word, any snarling from the pulpit, anything that is unkind, anything that is not loving, is therefore not of Christ.

This friendship of Christ we believe to be the gospel. I consider the attributes of the perfect friend to be: (1) that he knows all about us but still likes us, (2) that he would lay down his life for his friends, and (3) that he is always available and all-sufficient. Then, when I look at the life of Jesus of Nazareth, I see that He was absolutely this kind of Friend: (1) in His coming to live with His friends, in His whole ministry of friendship, (2) in His dying for His friends, and (3) in His return to His friends. And what I see Jesus of Nazareth doing in the gospel narratives, I believe the eternal Christ, the Spirit of Christ, to be doing in the twentieth century. Across the centuries and across the oceans the same spirit of Christ is still saying today as yesterday, "You are my friends: I am with you always." Here is true, reasonable, charismatic Christianity, God in the twentieth century, the friendship and the love of Christ.

This was my interpretation of the Gospel when I was first ordained; this was the gospel I falteringly propounded in my first sermon, on the very day of my ordination, after being dropped off at the vicarage with all the trepidation of a new boy starting at boarding school, and knowing about as much. My text was then "You are my friends", and it still is (when I start a sermon with a text). This is the gospel I have proclaimed, and I have tried to live with this, in companionship with steel-workers and tanners in Warrington, Lancs, dockers and typists in Bootle, businessmen and labourers in Liverpool, farmers in rural Ontario, chemical workers in Sarnia's chemical valley, tomato-growers in Essex County, and now the poor on Toronto's skid row. In that time, nearly forty years, almost everything has changed, including our theology. But the gospel of Christ's friendship has remained the same. Here, while most of my sermons have become outdated, this theme remains unchanged. It is the same eternal gospel of eternal love. I believe that today it may perhaps best be presented in terms of friendship and community.

When I was in a tough Lancashire town in my early ministry, I was quite stirred by Smart's *Christ on the Thames Embankment*, the story of the writer's work with the "down-and-outs" living on the Thames Embankment in London. With almost the same tenacity that I hold on to some of my Latin "tags", I have remembered two sayings in that book. They were spoken by men on London's skid row who were really up against life at the time. One said: "I will not allow circumstances to crush me, but let the spirit in me conquer them as Christ conquered the Cross. I like to think of Christ as my pal." The other, describing how he used to walk about crushed by the contemptuous way in which everyone looked at him in his old and ill-fitting clothes, said: "I used to long for the night to come to hear the voice of my only friend, Jesus Christ." I had never met these men; I believed their stories because of the obvious sincerity of the writer, and often spoke of them, but I had never met people quite like them. *But now I have.* On Toronto's skid row, which is largely my parish, I meet such people, and I know some of them would say the very same things. It is my pride and joy to meet and to know, to be enriched and encouraged by these men, who in desperate circumstances have made a friendship with Christ and found Him today their restorer and supporter in life.

Our Sunday worship is fairly simple, somewhat informal – as informal as it can be and still pass as an Anglican act of worship. But it is by no means sloppy. We have a fine organ, a three-manual Casavant instrument, which always adds dignity to the service. Since the worship part of our church is curtained off, we are bound to sit close together. This is an immediate aid to fellowship and intimacy, so much better than a scarcity of bodies draped over an illimitable stretch of pews fading off into the distant horizon. We have a choir, a rather mixed brew, at times up to twenty voices (or twenty-one if you count mine – I was never allowed to sing at school). There are boys and girls of all ages, teenagers, and two or three adults. Some of them can sing, some are ornamental, and some are neither, but a choir can be a very useful source of evangelism, as indeed can Servers and a Junior Chancel Guild, to create in young people a feeling of usefulness and involvement in the worship and activity of the church. The Sunday school sits with us, because the children are mostly of families (father *or* mother) that come to church. After a short time they are led out by the Cross, which is fairly new in this previous Protestantism preserve: the church managed to get on very well without the Cross for a number of years! To add to the intimacy of the church service, and for a feeling of communication, I no longer mount the pulpit, although it is quite a magnificent affair (anyhow, I have always felt that you can lead a preacher to the pulpit, but you can't make him preach). This is not from a sense of vertigo; it just seems somewhat odd, with a small and intimate congregation, to blast forth like Jupiter tossing his thunderbolts through aisle and apse, and belching forth broadsides of fire and brimstone all over the landscape. So I just sit on a chair on the chancel steps and talk to the folks. I think there is merit in this: it adds a sense of camaraderie. Several people have said they like it and feel they are being spoken *to*, not *at*. A Maritimer even told me it was the first church he had liked to be in.

The congregation is fairly small, numbering about fifty people but tending to increase. They are all poor. One male member of our congregation is fully employed if we do not count a volunteer who has recently come to help us. A few women have jobs, and one or two have husbands who work, but nearly everyone has a pension of some kind, old age, disability, etc. Rarely do we see a mother and father together. Nearly all our children have only one parent; almost every home has some marital breakdown or irregular relationship, though some common-law relationships are very faithful and would compare favourably with legal marriages in this respect.

A rough breakdown of the sixty or so people who come to our church, apart from children and the occasional member of the Board, is as follows: employed men, 2; employed women, 8; wives of employed men, 2; students (mostly male), 13; L.I.P. workers, 1; father's allowance, 2; mother's allowance, 2; private income, 1; teen-agers, 8; welfare, 13; old age pensioners, 12; disability pensioners, 4. Quite often there are more men than women. This is largely because we have a number of male students from Nigeria, and also because there are a great many single men in the district. Nearly every member of the congregation comes from our immediate district, or has recently moved to Ontario Housing fairly near, or is a West Indian who has moved to a better place but still comes back. Almost everyone lives in a state of crisis: there are problems of bad health of body and mind, alcohol, poverty, immigration, housing, unemployment, low intelligence, marital or domestic problems. Surely these are the people who need the church, and it is a privilege to be called to minister to and with them.

We try to throw some colour into our worship. Our Servers wear coloured cassocks (property of the Junior Chancel Guild), according to the season of the Church Year. At the Centennial, or some other special occasion, our children in very colourful costumes have carried excellently painted shields of the Anglican dioceses in Canada and elsewhere. (This is a routine we have often used in missionary pageants, Bible Society Centennials, etc., with up to 150 children of all races.) When we have been able, we have presented acts of Christian drama and pageantry. We have presented the short liturgical play of Easter (the Ludus Paschalis or "Quem Quacritis") and have assisted other churches, notably St. Paul's at Bloor Street, to do the same. On one occasion we presented the "Harrowing of Hell" (the Descent of

Christ to the Underworld – very appropriate for this part of Toronto) at All Saints' in the morning and again at St. Paul's in the evening.

We claim to have presented the first outdoor nativity play in Canada, and so far we have not been contradicted. This was a ten-minute play (short because of the cold) which we first put on at our parking-lot in Sherbourne Street – "Christ comes to Cabbagetown". It received a good deal of coverage from the press and TV. I would like to have borrowed a camel from the local zoo, but this might have been a bit too much for the local inhabitants – pink elephants and snakes perhaps, but hardly camels. We also presented the play in the grounds of the Moss Park High-Rise Apartment Project. This was simply done with a tape and amplifier, and a small cast suiting the actions to the words, and looked very effective from the fifteenth floor or so. Our audience watched from their high gallery seats, almost all round us, with Queen Street in the background. We repeated this one or two years, and then moved on to the Old City Hall on Queen Street, whose setting provides a magnificent stage for a play of this nature.

At Harvest Festival we no longer leave it to the holy women alone (God bless 'em) to do the decorating job on a Saturday afternoon. We all do this together on Harvest Sunday as an act of worship. Led by the choir and Sunday school, we all bring our gifts in a basket to the priest and lay them before the altar (as instructed in the Book of Deuteronomy), and we put all our goods around the chancel while we belt out the good old harvest hymns. So much more of this could be done if we had a few more capable people to carry it off. I am convinced that simple acts of liturgical drama, combined with the worship and as an integral part of the Eucharist, are of great benefit to the church and people, as indeed they were for so many centuries in the Church of the Middle Ages.

After the Sunday service, we have coffee and cookies. We gather round in the community part of the church to fraternize. This is a happy time, and completely refutes the line of the hymn, "O in what divers pains they met: O with what joy they went away", which I often have felt reflects the feelings of a normal congregation. Usually at this time someone in the congregation, or someone who drops in off the street, needs some special guidance, to be taken to the Detox Centre, or given a meal-ticket. It is becoming quite a job to get the people to go away, so that we may shut the doors (the only day when they do shut so early, which should make us think) in order to go home for dinner.

Our worship isn't quite like Westminster Abbey in quality of performance, nor is it comparable to that of the suburban churches where I have worked and worshipped, but it is at least equally sincere. It has also resulted in something that is quite remarkable in an Anglican Church, and in most other kinds of churches: *Poor people are beginning to feel at home in our church on Sunday*, to feel that they are part of the church, and that the church belongs to them.

CHAPTER IX

THE AGAPE SUPPER – A SECULAR COMMUNION

As we saw in the previous chapter, some few poor people do come to Sunday church. They form our Sunday congregation (though many are quite transient) and are beginning to feel at home in church. But we need simpler, far simpler, ways of worship for people who are quite out of touch with church services, some of whom may even be illiterate. I thought deeply about this matter, with a good deal of travail and an element of abandonment too, for even I used to like belting out the "Te Deum" to Stanford in B and singing snatches of Marbecke in the bathtub. It seemed to me, then, after a great deal of thought, that the whole idea of Christianity is community, "togetherness". So I asked myself: Where is it in ordinary life that we meet people, and what do we do when we get together? The answer seemed to be that at such times: (1) we like to eat together; (2) we like to talk and discuss together; (3) we like to sing and enjoy music and drama; and (4) we like to plan to help people in groups and service clubs.

Could an act of worship be built into and

around such activities? It seemed to me that these four things were in fact the very ingredients of apostolic worship, and of the early Christian *agape* (meaning "love" in its purest sense). The Agape Fellowship Meal was the remembrance of Jesus in the Breaking of the Bread – an act of worship, discussion, singing, fellowship, and charity. I decided to try out with my poor people a similar simple act of worship, in the manner of the early Christians. For my people might endure a sort of "religion without tears" in an atmosphere that was not holy or phony, but generally one of happy fellowship.

This has developed into our Agape Supper, which I sometimes call the "secular communion" (and which is sometimes also known as "Norman's un-holy communion"). It is well called the "secular communion"; I think Jesus meant the act of remembrance to be done at such a supper, very likely in a home, as the Jewish ritual fellowship-meals always were. It is even perhaps well called "un-holy", because it is natural and commonplace, a part of everyday life and a normal living relationship with Jesus Christ, and through Him with God and one another. This Agape Supper is, with the Open Door, one of the secular approaches that our church is making to people (I will write later of the varied forms it may take). It is our way of trying to be the Church in the world, to provide a simple happy act of worship without the misery of so much religion, and yet at the same time to provide a very real sacrament.

The scene of the Agape Supper is the Parish Hall. There is a top-table for the officiant and the servers, so that the actions of the Eucharist may be seen. The other tables are in horse-shoe formation on either side, with a few separate tables for families. This gives a mother or father a chance to control the children, and also to break bread for them, which is the way we think Jesus would have liked – in the home, rather than in the church. The families are really the people we most want, because this all started for us as a family night.

There is also a group of teenagers of the Junior Chancel Guild, who act as Servers. Then there are a few women, some of whom come to church, among them a good Roman Catholic and a few lonely people who enjoy company. Old people do not come to the Agape Supper much, for it can be dangerous to walk about at nights. There will be one or two mentally retarded or emotionally disturbed, a few common-law couples, and also quite a number of men from the local rooming-houses, some of whom we know very well, and occasionally a very tough-looking customer. Sometimes the leaders of the Children's Nursery and a few students come to look after the kids. Most of the children are of Sunday school families, and one or two fathers or mothers may come to church on Sundays too, such as a French Roman Catholic with his two half-Indian children. On the other hand, the leading lady who looks after the supper, and is about our best church-worker, says she has never felt comfortable in church on Sunday. Almost everyone is unemployed and mostly unemployable, so this outing is a happy time for them. Families who cannot afford a baby-sitter can all come out together. We have varied between a "pot-luck" supper and a planned meal, where everyone contributes a little – one dollar for a family and fifty cents for a single person. The average number will be about 45 adults and 20 children. There are a number of regular attenders, but also a floating element (as long as they float on the right liquid we are quite happy).

Following the supper, the children are cared for by students, the teenagers have a programme, some of the adults play cards; but a number – usually from twelve to eighteen, mostly men – come in for a Bible Study. This is on extremely simple lines, and we say what we feel: there's no holiness about it, no phoniness. If we don't accept something, we don't hesitate to say so. Either Ed, our former caretaker, or I usually act as the devil's advocate to make it more lively. It is the first Bible Class with which I have been connected where we have Roman Catholics, fundamentalists, a professed agnostic who knows the Bible better than anyone else, a cowboy singer from the local pubs, one or two disturbed people, and possibly someone under the influence of alcohol. But it is very sincere and sometimes humbling, when someone who has had very little chance in life obviously has a stronger faith than oneself. And best of all there is the spirit of "belonging", to which we have previously referred. There is a sense of community. I feel this so strongly when I look around at all these good people with their different backgrounds: "You who were not a people are now the people of God."

I believe that this weekly act of worship, held each Tuesday night in our Parish Hall at supper-time, is one of great blessing. I believe that Jesus is there in the Spirit with us as much as in the church building itself. I have no real desire that after a time these people will graduate to coming to church on Sunday. Why should they? Would it be a graduation? Is it any better? Why should I push for them to come to something apart from life, instead of staying with something which is a part of ordinary life? I don't care if Jesus is in the elements: He is there in the Spirit. I also think that, although we are in a peculiar place, and Lord knows we are a peculiar lot of people, such worship as this would be a great benefit in other places I have been, and in the life and worship of many other churches of all types.

As Boyd states in *The Underground Church:*

> . . . one experiences in an Underground Church a true sense of belonging. Unlike the average parish in which neither the priest nor the other parishioners are likely to know one another's name, in an Underground Church all the members soon know one another on a first-name basis and are willing to share their thoughts and souls with one another . . . . A true sense of brotherhood in the Lord is experienced intensely in the eucharistic meal. An experience of the presence of the Spirit of Jesus in the midst of His followers is inevitable in this intimate setting. The binding force which the Spirit provides becomes the source of community. . . . The Community *is* the Church.[1]

This I know to be true from the experience of followship in the Bible Study, which follows right after the supper; there is a sense of belonging, a

---

[1] Malcolm Boyd, *The Underground Church* (New York: Sheed & Ward, 1968), p. 131.

finding of community. Symanowski speaks of "a congregation springing up and a Church being established".[2] This has been our experience at All Saints'. I find the true Church in the setting of the people of our Supper and Bible Study Groups.

It is quite remarkable that, in the well-known text "Behold I stand at the door and knock" (Rev. 3:20), Jesus says: "If any man open the door, I will come in and *have supper with him*." Surely in this and in the post-resurrection appearances of Jesus at supper, there is something very special – something in the supper together which in the Eucharist alone, without the Agape, we cannot help missing however hard we try.

The Origin of the Eucharist in the Chaburah Meal

I would like to give a more careful expression of the history of the Agape meal, as far as we may know it, and discuss its validity in the life and practice of the early Church. Gregory Dix, in his monumental *The Shape of the Liturgy*,[3] points out that the Last Supper was evidently a Jewish religious meal, a chaburah supper, the meeting of a group of friends (*chaberim*). This group would meet together weekly to share supper, generally on the eve of Sabbaths or holy days; each would contribute to the meal, and they would enjoy companionship and recreation, probably with a religious background. At such a chaburah meal, the

---

[2] Horst Symanowski, *The Christian Witness in an Industrial Society*, translated by George H. Kehm (Philadelphia: Westminster Press, 1964), p. 54.

[3] Dom Gregory Dix, *The Shape of the Liturgy* (London: Westminster, 1945), p. 30ff.

leader would take bread, break it with set words, and each member, following him, would share a fragment of the loaf. The meal followed, and also a hand-washing; then came the "berakah", the blessing or thanksgiving over the cup from which all sipped. The ceremony ended with a Psalm.

This is the Jewish background of the Last Supper. As Dix says:

> It is a chaburah supper such as our Lord and His disciples were accustomed to hold regularly, held on this occasion twenty-four hours before the Passover of that year.[4]

Here, then, at this meal in the Upper Room on the eve of the Passover, in the city of Jerusalem, is held the weekly meeting of Jesus' group, but with an atmosphere of unusual excitement and charged with emotion. Jesus gives thanks for the bread. The words are not recorded, because every Jew knows them by heart ("Blessed be Thou, O Lord our God, eternal King, Who bringest forth bread from the earth"). He then distributes to His friends and adds the somewhat enigmatic words (only later perhaps to become intelligible): "This is my Body which is given for you. Do this for the re-calling of me" (I Cor. 11:24). Dix points out that there is no reason to tell them to do this, because this was their normal custom: what is new is the expression "in remembrance of me". When they do this in the future, it will be in remembrance of the leader with whom they are now sharing their chaburah for the last time.

After this comes the foot-washing, which Jesus

---

4 Ibid., p. 30ff.

substitutes for the usual hand-washing, and which He elects to do Himself as an act of humility and as an example (John 13:15). Then comes the Thanksgiving or berakah, the long benediction said over the cup of water mixed with wine. The words of Thanksgiving would be the regular ones, referring to the old covenant of God with Israel. They all partake of the cup in the customary manner and, while the cup is passing, Jesus adds the startling words: "This cup is the new covenant in my blood. Do this whenever you drink it, for the re-calling of me" (I Cor. 11:25). Here again, the command to drink (like that of eating) is nothing new: it is only the extra saying about the "new covenant in my blood" that is new. In Dix's words:

> What our Lord did at supper then, was not to establish any new rite. He attached to the two corporate acts which were sure to be done when His disciples met in the future – *the only two things which He could be sure they would do together regularly in any case* – a quite new meaning, which had a special connection with His own impending death.[5]

It seems that here, in Gregory Dix's account of the Last Supper as a form of the chaburah, is a clue to the rediscovery of true Christian worship for today. Indeed, one might wonder how what we sometimes do on Sunday could possibly have originated from the Last Supper: it has gone so far from the original setting. A good argument could be raised for the theory that a well-conducted weekly supper-meeting of a Rotary Club is nearer

---

[5] Ibid., p. 30ff.

in form, and perhaps in spirit, to the Last Supper than are many of our church services!

The picture of the worship of the Primitive Church is fairly clear from Acts 2:42.7, I Corinthians 11, the *Didache*, and writings of the early Fathers. The first Church of Christ, the friends of Jesus, met as they used to do during His life, as His club, His chaburah, but now they especially remembered the words of commemoration which He added to their usual meal, the words about His body being given for them and about the cup of the new covenant. They continued as they always did at the chaburah meal, but now it was in remembrance of Jesus. They were joyful, remembering, more than His death, His glorious Resurrection: why should they not eat their meal with exultation (Acts 2:46)?

As followers of Christ, the Christian chaburah continued to meet in various houses, in the setting of a meal, with the special moment being the blessings (eulogies) over the bread and the cup, the breaking and the sharing now in remembrance of their departed leader. Added to this would be discussion of the new faith (the doctrine of the apostles) and the *koinonia*, which meant not so much brotherly fellowship, although this would be natural and evident, but a sharing of gifts and care of the needy. This simple act was to develop into the Christian Eucharist. It was so obviously within the setting of a meal. They had always met like this during the life of Jesus; they had met with Him like this at the Last Supper; they had met with Him like this at His first appearance in His risen life. Here was the obvious pattern for their worship as His friends in remembrance of Him.

By the beginning of the second century, however, it would appear that a divorce in the Lord's Supper had come about. (This was due partly to disorders, sometimes present in the fellowship-meal, which Paul so severely castigates in I Corinthians 11:20 – and with which we have to contend occasionally at All Saints' – and partly to a difficulty in handling the fellowship-meal with a large assembly in such places as Rome.) The Eucharist (the Thanksgiving apart from the Agape or chaburah meal) became the liturgical worship of the ecclesia or large assembly of the Church, as Dix points out. The Agape continued *along with* the Eucharist, but *apart from* it, held at a different time and place. Ignatius speaks of them as distinct, and by the end of the second century Tertullian in the West and Clement of Alexandria in the East speak of the Agape as a technical term for the fellowship meal *apart* from the Eucharist.[6]

Thus, with the separation of the Eucharist and the Agape, we lost something of the original spirit of the chaburah meal. With the later building of large and spectacular churches, and the adornment of the Eucharist, we were well on the way to a perversion, or unusual emphasis, of the original act of worship. The Eucharist was more suited than a real meal for celebration in a noble basilica. Soon the Eucharist was to become the possession of a particular priesthood rather than of a "royal priest-

---

[6] Ibid., p. 79 and 100, quoting Ignatius: Smyrn., viii (A.D. 115).

hood" (I Peter 2:9). Robes and the salutations of
the imperial court replaced the simplicity of the
Upper Room, till the worship was honoured for
itself. There was less and less participation by the
laity in receiving the sacrament; despite all efforts
of Roman bishops and Protestant reformers very
few people received the sacrament in any regular
manner until the last century or two.

Restoring the Agape

Can not our present-day Christian worship reflect
more clearly the early Eucharist? When the friends
of Jesus, which we call His Church, meet together
for worship, the whole setting and atmosphere
might be centred around a meal, preferably a real
one, at the Lord's Table. As with the first followers of Jesus, there would be worship and remembrance, opportunities for inspiration and instruction.
There would be *koinonia* – fellowship, sharing and
service. This would be the Lord's Supper of which
St. Paul speaks (I Cor. 11:20), where the Eucharist is
combined with the Agape or love-feast.

This simple service of the Breaking of Bread
(which I venture to call the "secular communion"
because its place is out in the world, rather than in
the sanctuary) might take place at the beginning of
a meal of a small Christian group, for instance a
brotherhood, servers, or altar guild, instead of the
rather formal "grace". It might well sanctify an
afternoon meal of a senior citizens' meeting, as on
Maunday Thursday, when the gospel story might
be read and the Last Supper almost re-enacted.
(Does it matter whether one uses wafers or hot-
cross buns?) It could take place at a church-

meeting with lunch after the morning service. In many places it could replace the dull, formal, and often "gutless" Sunday service. Or such a service could go along with our present normal Communion; those who like the traditional liturgy could have this service, while others who do not like formality, who do not rise to the heights of the full Mass or have perhaps grown out of it, might have some simple Agape-Communion. The two kinds of worship might co-exist happily side by side, even as some churches presently indulge in both Low and High Mass. It comes simply to this: *Ubi Christus, ibi ecclesia.*

Such an Agape Supper has been our regular practice on Tuesday evenings for over two years, with a break for summer; we are now in our third season. We have simplified a little the form of liturgy given (a suggested form of service appears in the appendix), for the people who come are far from well-educated or religiously inclined. In a setting where more mature Christians are gathered, a great deal may be added without losing the effectiveness, and large numbers of people may be involved. Choirs could participate; there could be acts of drama and music, speakers. We have the custom of bringing the elements to the table for the eucharistic prayer; this is done by girls of the Chancel Guild who distribute them to the people at the tables. On festive occasions, such as Christmas, they have worn coloured cassocks, or costumes of pageantry. (But then, of course, if we are not careful, in our human weakness we will be adding the trappings of ecclesiasticism once more!)

Usually, to fill in the time during the movements

of distribution, when people might become restive, we sing a hymn, though we try to get one of not too churchy a flavour. Some of our men would like us to sing "Shall We Gather at the River?" or "Where Is My Wandering Boy To-night?" but we have carefully misplaced the music. We often sing such hymns as "Crimond", the hymn set to the "Londonderry Air", "Fairest Lord Jesus", or the hymn set to "John Brown's Body", which has attained a certain amount of respectability with Anglicans after being used at the funeral of Winston Churchill!

A large loaf of bread might be used, with pieces broken from it to emphasize the oneness of our fellowship; we have done this, but some prefer the more hygienic method of taking plates of broken bread to the tables, rather than allowing a great deal of handling. We use separate glasses, and grape-juice because of the liquor laws in Canada and the danger of even the smell of alcohol to some of us. In the small groups, however, one cup which all share may be more meaningful. On our particular pitch we lack a little of the propriety and sense of order that might be found in a more educated society and more stable neighbourhood, but at least we are on the way: "And they continued in the apostles' teaching and in fellowship, in the breaking of the bread and in prayer" (Acts 2:42).

CHAPTER X
ALL SAINTS' MEN'S CLUB

For some years before the "Friendship Centre" came to us, we had operated a Coffee-House of our own in the Parish Hall. The idea of course was borrowed from the Friendship Centre which was at the time meeting in a disused pub on Gerrard Street. We opened the Parish Hall two mornings a week and one evening, Tuesday, when the Friendship Centre was closed.

At first we found we couldn't even give the coffee away. Probably the men were afraid of the church offering gifts. However, after we advertised at Seaton House and elsewhere with the caption "NO GAMBLING, NO POLITICS, NO RELIGION", men began to come in, till ultimately, with perhaps a hundred men and unlimited cups of coffee, we couldn't pour it out fast enough. Our chief worker was our caretaker, Ed, who is presently acting as a part-time social worker in our church. We also had volunteers from the Brotherhoods of St. Timothy's (North Toronto) and of St. John's (York Mills). Here we first met some of the future directors of All Saints'.

This Coffee-House was an attempt to do our bit

at All Saints' in serving the needs of the single displaced men of the inner city, most of whom live in or near our parish. Generally there was very little disorder, and most of the men really seemed to appreciate our efforts to be friendly. We were able to assist quite a bit with clothing and footwear, and with the usual problems of finding overnight accomodation, relief, etc. We made good friends with the management and quite a few of the residents of Seaton House, the men's hostel run by the city. Out of the hundreds of men whom we saw over a few years, we could number about thirty or forty whom we came to know on terms of quite close friendship, and we felt they trusted us.

When the Friendship Centre moved into our Parish Hall in the fall of 1970, using the Hall almost every afternoon and evening, we no longer felt it our responsibility to keep open our smaller Coffee-House. But it seemed desirable that we should continue some activities with the group of men who had become our friends. We had already set aside two afternoons a week for cards, bingo, pool, and TV, and with the coming of the Friendship Centre we moved these activities into the basement of the Baldwin Hall. When the Mental Health Clinic moved into the Baldwin Hall, we shared our afternoons with the patients, and had a very happy time. We were able to provide coffee, cookies, and cakes, also sample packets of cigarettes to about thirty or forty men. There was always a friendly spirit, but in no way a feeling that this was charity. I have always looked at this as a kind of cross between the Granite Club and the Salvation Army. We ran a pool competition, but never finished, partly because we couldn't get two of the competitors sober on the same day.

This pattern served well for some time, till we began to get too many people coming in. It was in danger of becoming a "drop-in" rather than a club, and we were anxious to keep the club spirit. We felt that we could only know a limited number of people well on a friendly basis, and we were aiming to establish a more intimate group of friends rather than a nondescript mass. We therefore changed our plan and instead began to meet for lunches or supper once a week. This is our present pattern; each Wednesday, except in summer, about twenty-five of us have a good dinner together at noon. We are looked after by two women volunteers who do a fine job and are well regarded by the men.

We begin dinner with a ritual breaking of the bread, a quite short sacramental act, which I use instead of grace. I feel I can "do the Eucharist" easily and naturally this way, whereas to get up and say a few pious words or sing a hymn would seem phony and forcing the pace. The breaking of the bread sanctifies and re-inforces our fellowship, for there is a lovely spirit of warmth and happiness here. One highlight was an interview televised by the C.B.C. and also by the Downtown Community TV. Another time we had a visit from the retired Bishop of the Yukon. He felt very much at home; probably he thought he was back in the saloon with a bunch of prospectors in Dawson City. He led us in singing "Alouette", while one man played the piano and another produced his inevitable mouth-organ. This did more for the popularity of the episcopate than a whole broadside of sermons, and never were bishops in such favour since the time when they were released from the Tower of London in the seventeenth century.

Let me introduce you to some of my friends in the Men's Club. There is "Happy", as everyone calls him, one of the best-known figures in Cabbagetown. He has been an amputee for years, and he walks down from Fudger House (Senior Citizens' Nursing Home) nearly every day on his two artificial legs, using a pair of crutches. He always carries a mouth-organ which he will play with the least provocation. We used to find it hard to control his enthusiasm on a Sunday morning at church. Happy is a firm Christian, a very friendly character, and is almost the only man I know around here who doesn't drink. He has known a good deal of hardship; once he was living in an awful rooming-house (even judged by Cabbagetown standards; there was a warning on the door about entering "at your own risk"), and nearly died through neglect, being unable to look after himself properly. But he has always kept true to his chosen name: we honour Happy as one of the "triumphs of grace".

Leonard is a huge man in every possible place where one can be large. He wears a cowboy hat, which fits in with his character as a singer of western songs at the local saloons. Very friendly, very generous, very out-going, he has become a regular attender at the Agape Supper, the Open Door, and other activities, and even a regular worshipper at church on Sundays. He came from a good home, as pictures of his childhood show.

Jean is a French Canadian, formerly Roman Catholic, who brings his two half-Indian children to church each Sunday. He has bought them all bicycles and has a great time with them. He lives on Father's Allowance, as he is not in good health. We tell him he is lucky, he has his kids to look after and something to live for.

Jim is one of my very good friends. Since he left a respectable home, his life has been cursed by excess of alcohol. The danger comes when, after working, he is apt to blow his money and get really drunk. Unlike many, he doesn't really want to drink; I think he is quite serious about wanting to stop. He has told me he is really scared, for not only does he see snakes but they talk back to him. He is scared even when he is drinking, but he cannot stop. We hope he can pull through, although he has already injured his health and mind to some extent. Yet he still has one of the loveliest smiles, which comes from a good heart and a loving spirit.

Jeff is almost the same. He was once a skilled electronics craftsman. He is still able to work at odd jobs, and he almost refuses to live on welfare, but I can see he is getting more and more lost every year, and is not able to keep up as he did years ago. The breaking-point will come soon, and we don't know which way he will go.

Ken is just a normal elderly pensioner, who obviously enjoys spending a lot of time here and in the Friendship Centre. He is so pleased that he has just got a lovely new room in the Senior Citizens' Ontario Housing. There are quite a number of men like Ken around whose only fault is that they have had too many birthdays. We are very glad if we can make their lives brighter.

Carl is one of the salt of the earth, a grandfather

with a somewhat military cut to his jib. He goes to nearly all the men's clubs around, takes a Bible Class at Scott Mission, and helps with ours at the Agape Supper. He spends his retirement in this wonderful way giving himself and his time to the other men, who are not so fortunately balanced as himself. He is one of the leaders at our Men's Club.

Norman came to us for a short time to help us with preparing our dinners. He seemed a rather superior sort of chap, but again the problem was drink. Then we missed him for a time, till one day his family from Montreal came in to tell us he had died. He had been found in his own room a week after he had died, the place full of empty wine-bottles. He had told his family all about our club, and they were so grateful that they gave us all his furniture.

It has been a comfort to us to feel that we have done something to make the last years of a few men's lives happier by our club and our friendship. Thus far, out of the chaotic mass of single solitary lonely souls on and off skid row, we have a happy fellowship of good men, and up to a point a Christian fellowship. We are making friends; we are, I believe, meeting Christ in one another, the vision transparent in some, perhaps a little clouded in others. We are getting to feel closer to one another, forming something of a feeling of community. We are in touch with men who have been separated from "church" and organised religion for years; we are able to share with them a simple act of worship and at the same time show that we care.

Of course, we have a lot further to go yet, but we have lately made what I think is a real leap forward.

We were encouraged to start a Talk-Time before lunch, which has now developed into a Bible Study, not too formal and certainly not pious. About fifteen men come here, and the group enlarges as time gets nearer to dinner. Right now we are ploughing through St. Mark. It took years before I could come to this. This may have been my English shyness towards "religion", or it may have been the *gentle* leading of the Holy Spirit. Perhaps both contributed to common-sense.

Here, then, are the main elements of apostolic worship, as described in the early chapters of Acts – the Breaking of the Bread, the fellowship, the reading of the scriptures, charity – all are here in a simple way at our dinner. In this fellowship I believe that we now have a true Church – one of our three churches at All Saints' – that is, Sunday morning worship, Tuesday Agape, and now the Men's Club.

CHAPTER XI
THE FRIENDSHIP CENTRE

From the kitchen of the church a door leads into the Parish Hall. We open this and reel almost in shock at the prospect before us. Perhaps because it is unexpected in a church; suddenly we enter a world of noise, voices, clamour, and masses of bodies which gradually emerge through a pall of tobacco smoke. Is this a tavern? Can it be the stately hall of an old Anglican church?

When our eyes become accustomed to the smoke, and we have recovered our balance a little, we see perhaps two hundred of the toughest and in some ways the saddest men in Canada. Most are sitting down playing cards; two or three are playing different pianos and different tunes; some are trying to listen to the radio; a few are singing, even dancing, like an ex-commando friend of mine who once celebrated Christmas by dancing solo in the snow in Allen Gardens. Elsewhere a couple are quarrelling or arguing; a few are not sober and some are sleeping, oblivious to all around them. And at the same time a volunteer is listening to someone tell the story of his life, in an inebriated condition and with a strong Scottish or European accent.

I have seen women shrink at this sight like petunias in the frost; I have seen strong men quail in amazement when first suddenly confronted with this spectacle. I remember how an elderly member of our Board, our architect, who emerged from the basement into the large hall, was narrowly missed by a flying chair, and then, faced by the sight of a man lying in a pool of blood (actually there was more blood than injury), exclaimed, "My God, get me out of here!" Strong words for a Leaside church warden, but not remarkable. And this was one of the more friendly moments at the Friendship Centre!

If we get courage and go in, we meet some of the best people in the world, volunteers, dedicated men and women serving coffee, talking and counselling the men. Then – if we are at all out-going and not too shy – we have a cup of coffee, go sit with someone, and begin to chat. Of course, there is quite often a crisis situation, or something unexpected may occur, but when we get to know a few of the chaps, we begin to feel at home, make friends, and enjoy the privilege of service.

The Friendship Centre began in 1964. As was mentioned before, it operated for quite a time in a disused pub at the corner of Gerrard and Jarvis streets, before moving to the Parish Hall at All Saints'. The organization has been jointly sponsored by Holy Trinity and St. Luke's (United) churches, and supported by various charities including the Diocese of Toronto Outreach. Bill Stevens was director, assisted by a deaconness, Leslie Dampier; Frances Bowman is presently in charge, assisted by a group of volunteers and an active Board led by Professor Michael Powicke. The volunteers come from all over the city and are of varying creeds and nationalities, but they are united in the same common purpose, the extension of the right hand of fellowship to their less fortunate fellow-citizens. So, though All Saints' can in no way claim any credit for the Friendship Centre (we wish we could), we are very proud and happy to have this organization and these people with us in our buildings, sharing the total operation of outreach and friendship to the community in which we commonly serve.

The Centre may entertain three hundred men in an afternoon and evening in winter, perhaps even more. In a single month, tea or coffee is served to as many as 8,000 people. During 1970, 63,000 cups of coffee were served, referrals to established agencies numbered 536 people, 954 articles of clothing were distributed, and 235 over-night accomodations were found. I received these figures from an article in the *Telegram*, which goes on to say:

> The whole idea is to show that somebody cares, that these people are not forgotten. There is no fixed program, but there are summer picnics and Christmas parties. Rules and regulations are few – friendship is the thing.
>
> The success of the project from the very beginning has been measured in terms of human values, as it is in these terms that the Centre is making its contribution to the community. Four important elements contribute to the viability of the undertaking: members, staff, volunteers, and contributions. . . .
>
> Acceptance is most important to these people, because so many of them feel lost, lonely, rejected by society. The Centre aims to provide this, as well as dealing with special problems and referring men

> to suitable agencies and other sources of aid. . . . It
> is well named the "Friendship Centre".[1]

Helen Boyd, who is one of the original volunteers
and helps keep the Friendship Centre open every
Christmas Day, tells us that the men feel it is their
own place. "They have many stories," she has said,
"of their experiences in wars which took them to
many parts of the world. We know of some of the
hardships and disabilities they are still suffering. One
man has a steel plate in his forehead, is blind in one
eye, and deaf in one ear. Another has shrapnel
lodged in his back and one arm. Others are lame and
otherwise handicapped.

"Other men have suffered from accidents in their
civilian life. One of them was in a car accident and
lost a finger and thumb and had a collapsed lung,
but he did not charge the nineteen-year-old youth,
because he had a crippled mother to care for.
Another had a truck fall on him and was in hospital
for six months and in Riverdale after that.

"There are a number of epileptics who belong to
the Friendship Centre. A schizophrenic who used to
come in every day is now living in a house run by
Queen Street Mental Health Centre. He is getting
proper meals and there is companionship there
which he did not have when living in one room. He
was doing part-time work the last time we saw him
and seems much happier.

"A number of the men have moved to a better
area. Several are being cared for in nursing-homes
or hostels. A few are enjoying apartments in city

[1] Wilson McConnell, "Oasis of Friendship", in Toronto *Telegram*,
March 20, 1971.

housing; but there are still many living in one room, sometimes a very drab setting, and for these and the unemployed the Friendship Centre is a place where they can spend a few hours of an otherwise empty day."

Many more stories could be told of the lives and experiences of the guests at the Friendship Centre, but we will only give three of them, as reported by Patricia Clarke in the United Church *Observer* (March 1973):

> One day a man heard the sound of a piano as he shuffled by. He came in, sat down and played Beethoven's Moonlight Sonata and Brahm's Lullaby as [Mrs. Bowman, the director] had never heard them. After each, he stood and bowed from the waist: "For you, dear lady." "He used to be a concert pianist", she said. "Now he is an alcoholic. He sits all day in Allan Gardens and the children kick at him and spit on him. But here he was a person who could play for a lady."
>
> But another day it was a young man who slouched up to the table where she was helping volunteers serve coffee and stuck a knife against her stomach. "I'm going to kill somebody," he said. While a volunteer edged out to the telephone, Mrs. Bowman said calmly, "What for? You come and sit down and tell me all about it." When the police arrived, they found a young man sitting beside a motherly little lady, earnestly telling her his troubles. They asked for his knife, and he had forgotten where he had put it.
>
> Still another day a newcomer immediately became the centre of a disturbance. (Mrs. Bowman has learned a lot about getting in the middle of a group fast, to keep a pleasant afternoon from ending in a near-riot.) This time the newcomer was direct from . . . penitentiary, out in society for the first time in 17 years. Fifteen minutes later she had

him at the piano, bellowing out "The Old Rugged Cross".

These are some of the days and some of the people who come to the Friendship Centre. We honour the workers there for their demonstration of love and concern for some of Canada's lonely and forgotten people. We are proud to have them on the team with us.

CHAPTER XII

"AHBENOOJEYUG" – THE CANADIAN INDIAN CHILDREN'S PROGRAMME

The area around All Saints' is largely Anglo-Saxon. In fact, Cabbagetown has always been an Anglo-Saxon stronghold (or ghetto), if in this category we include the traditional enemies of the English, namely the Irish, Welsh and Scots. But there are other nationalities too. There are a number of Chinese, probably the best citizens in Toronto, with whom, regrettably, we have had very little contact. With the newer West Indians we have had very happy relations: for one thing, they play cricket, and you can't play cricket and not be a gentleman. The West Indians and the Guyanese greatly enrich the church life of All Saints', and of many other Metro churches. There are, of course, many migrants from the Maritimes, who help to maintain a British tradition (though I wish we had a specially detailed Maritime clergyman to care for these migrants, for they are often quite unhappy).

However, a large element of the population migrant to Toronto are our native Canadian Indians. According to the Union of Ontario Indians, there are some 20,000 Indians in the city, and some 9,000 between Yonge Street and the Don River. This means that a good number live in the area of All Saints', and come within the area of our concern. Many of them are single men who have sunk to the level of the Anglo-Saxon skid row "drop-out". There are some Indian women; and it is a sad, but not unknown, sight to see a white or Indian drunk with an Indian woman trailing a yard or two behind, as though in some form of captivity or subjection. There are also single-parent families (as are nearly all our families) and they are rather poor.

A number of young Indian people are drawn to the city, much as the migrants from the Maritimes or from Northern Ontario, seeking a fuller life than they may find on the reserve, desiring a better education, or just looking for something to do. The life of the young Indian here is not too different from that of the young farm boy in the big city, except that it is a little more difficult after living on the reserve. Teenagers, we are told, find it difficult in the city, especially if they are short of money; a number end up on the streets. There is also a feeling of estrangement; young Indians have said that the authorities are inclined to pick on them; they feel conscious of being watched. Some fail to understand their own identity and culture, and have said that they would rather not be Indians because of the trouble it causes them.

Some time ago we became aware of the number of Indians around us. It had seemed to me that the traditional sending of baskets and bales to the Indian reserves and missions was not all that should be done. Too long have we sung in Sunday school such songs as "Jesus loves the Indian boy; bow and arrow for a toy", while we have forgotten all about his alcoholic father on Sherbourne Street. There are probably as many Canadian Indians in our parish as on some of the reserves in northern Saskatchewan. These Indians around us are our parishioners, though they may not like to be so called; it seemed to me that we should be concerned about so large a group, especially when they speak our language after being untaught their own tongue at the residential school – a fact that they do not so easily forget.

We realized that local Indians in need would more likely be helped by people of their own race and culture, so we visited the Indian Centre at Beverley Street and the Union of Ontario Indians to offer the use of our buildings. I was at this time quite anxious that a branch or eastern depot of the Indian Centre be set up at All Saints', for so many of the people never went across Yonge Street. We also thought that perhaps an Indian Family Night might be operated at All Saints' in the Parish Hall. One or two beginnings were made. Two Indian students worked with us to provide in the mornings a Coffee-House for Indians, but without any marked success. Then Alec, an Indian councellor from the Union of Ontario Indians, worked with us for a year, keeping quite busy with legal matters, which were his particular concern. During the summer we welcomed a group of seventeen Indian students, who, under good supervision, studied legal matters and made a research-study of the district. All these efforts were perhaps rather abortive, but from them we established a friendly relationship and, I think, a feeling of trust and credibility with the Indian groups. In many of these groups, the personnel had experienced only unhappy contact with the white men in the residential schools of the past.

It was therefore with great happiness that we received a request for space in our buildings from a L.I.P. (Local Initiatives Program) group to set up an office for the Indian Big Brothers. This was to be an Indian branch of the well-known Big Brother organization. The Big Brother concept is based on the one-to-one relationship of child and adult, and is intended to help children who come from single-parent families or from families with problems. Children are referred to the organization by the Children's Aid, by schools and by parents. Visits to schools and parents are made, and the Big Brother (or Sister) is carefully screened. Then the couple, child and adult, is fixed up. The Indian Big Brothers group is under the umbrella of the Metro organization, and their programme is designed to apply this concept to the Indian youngster in the city, who needs not only an adult friend, but also somebody to provide a positive Indian adult model. It is hoped that these children will see Indian people doing well in the world, who are proud of being Indians, and then get to know such persons as their friends. The Big Brother is almost always an Indian himself, and many children of mixed racial parentage are involved in the programme. To this movement a Big Sister group was later added.

A second application came to us to house the workers of a Concerned Native Citizens' Children's Programme, who have now been with us about a year. (For a short time we also housed a Native Alcohol and Drug Addiction Centre, but recently they have moved to proper premises at the Addiction Research Foundation.) The Big Brothers, the Big Sisters, and the Children's Programme have since merged into one group. They have had a staff of over twenty, so that at times when all are here it almost looks as though the Indians are taking over! "Ahbenoojeyug", Ojibway for "children", is the title given to the combined programme.

A large aim of the programme is to develop in the children an interest in their own culture, and a feeling of pride in their racial background. History and literature have been unkind in their treatment of the Indian; here is a serious attempt to give a reasonable and well-deserved national pride, yet within the Canadian mosaic. The goals have been clearly set forward: (1) to establish a comprehensive programme for native children in the city of Toronto providing social, cultural, recreational, and educational programmes and supporting services; (2) to facilitate the development of the native community, both adults and children, through leadership training and development of a positive cultural identity by establishing priorities and implementing solutions; and (3) to promote cross-cultural understanding.

As many as two hundred children are presently involved in the programmes, and the number is growing. The age range is from five to sixteen years, with older children being trained as junior leaders. Two adjacent downtown churches provide the necessary space for activities and provision of an evening meal. (Alas, All Saints' had not the unoccupied space to offer for these activities.) The children are transported by streetcar or by one or two vans, while buses are chartered for special trips such as to the Annual Pow-wow at Walpole Island, and shortly, it is hoped, to Birch Island.

There is an After-School Programme that is cultural, educational, social, and recreational. Children are exposed to their own culture as well as to others which make up the "Canadian fabric". As a report from the staff leaders states, the children will

> ... participate in sports, such as baseball, hockey, lacrosse, and Indian hand-games. Educational and cultural activities, such as home economics, Indian dancing, drumming, and singing, Native languages, arts and crafts, drama and film will be included. Trips will be organized so that the children can learn about their environment through travel. They will visit places of interest in the city ... so that they will have a better understanding of city life and make use of its resources.
>
> Trips to reserves will help the children to understand the ways of their people and will give them a better insight into their own heritage. As most of the children will be coming to the programme directly from school, we will be providing one nourishing meal a day to offset any dietary deficiencies they may have at home.

During summer, a daytime programme will replace an after-school one, with special emphasis on swimming, camping, canoeing, and outdoor as well as cultural activities. There is training for leaders as well as tutoring of students by volunteers who are usually university students. In view of the large drop-out rate of children from school, a special emphasis will be placed on encouraging children to go on to a profession. National pride is cultivated by Indian dancing, visits to pow-wows, and instruction in Indian games, such as lacrosse and cocoosh. It is hoped in the programme to draw on the skills of well-known Indian celebrities, orators, singers, folk-dancers, poets, film-makers, story-tellers, and perhaps there may be opportunities to meet some of these celebrities face to face.

CHAPTER XIII

DUNDAS DAY-CARE – "HEALING TO THEM THAT ARE BRUISED"

Very early we had realized the need for a psychologist around our church, as well as legal aid advisors and all sorts of experienced and qualified counsellors, if we were to do a real job where we were. Perhaps we had thought of new buildings with offices for all such services. In any event, Queen Street Hospital had begun operations in a church situated near to them, and we were fortunate to approach the hospital at a time when they too were thinking of moving out into the world. In November 1969, I received a letter from the Chief of Eastern Services at the hospital, in reply to one of mine:

> I can well imagine the many people who come to you and the varied problems they present. Your idea about having a psychiatrist at your offices is a good one, but whether this is feasible, I can't at this point answer.

Recent years, in Toronto at least, have seen a great move in this direction: storefront clinics, storefront dentists, storefront lawyers and doctors. The tendency is to "outreach", or missionary extension – to meet people where they are, or half-way, before the crisis comes, before the pressure mounts too high; prevention if possible before need of cure. This also fits in with the present-day tendency to avoid the "institution" where possible, and meet people as "clients" in small groups and centres rather than as "cases" in the atmosphere of the large and possibly impersonal institution.

At all events, within a year from my writing, and following frequent visits from the staff of the hospital, Queen Street Hospital decided to move in. (I suspect that, after looking around for a suitable place, they met me and the wardens of the church and thought that nowhere were they so needed!) A further letter of 18 August 1970 from the Eastern Services Chief of Queen Street Hospital proposed that "initially the programme begin with approximately 10-12 patients. The focus of the programme would be one of assimilating these people into the community. Most of them have had a history of social isolation and of depending upon institutions. Our goal will be to move the patients from the hospital to the Day Centre, and from there into the community, using the many agencies and resources in the community to provide the socialization and support the patients require."

So towards the end of 1970 the operation began under the name of the Dundas Day-Care Centre, with the object being, in layman's language, to care for patients who were too good for the hospital but perhaps not good enough to be on their own in the outside world. I have myself met in the Coffee-House a former patient of a mental hospital released into the jungle of life in the inner city – alone in the streets all day, sleeping in the herd at night in the city hostel – alone when he wanted company, in company when he wanted to be alone! It was to meet this sort of situation that the Dundas Day-Care Centre was set up. During this time with us it has grown to about twenty-five patients (or "clients") who meet there regularly, with other people visiting. The staff personnel include two full-time nurses, two part-time nurses, a psychologist, a social worker, a visiting doctor, a chaplain, students, and volunteers. They are able to receive people who come to them in need, or whom we and other agencies transfer to their expert attention. And at times of crisis, how fortunate is a clergyman who is able to take someone whom he cannot expertly help to a staff of built-in nurses and doctor!

The work of the Centre, programme and philosophy, is well-expressed in a report issued in March 1971, entitled *The First Four Months of Operation*. This report describes the programme as including a one-hour general business meeting of staff and clients each morning, at which plans are made for the day and any problems of the Centre are discussed. A break for gym activities or relaxation is followed by two one-hour therapy groups led by a psychologist and a nurse. Afternoons are spent carrying out the basic objectives, and also guiding clients through crisis periods and problems of day-to-day living. Volunteers offer their services for kitchen, clerical, and janitorial duties.

The philosophy behind the operation has four basic aims:

(1) To provide a community extension of the therapeutic "power-sharing milieu" of the hospital.

Here, each member has the democratic right of an equal voice in all decisions relative to the life of the Centre. He has also the right to be accepted unconditionally as an "individual with inherent dignity and self-worth". He is encouraged to express his own opinions freely and to take the initiative himself. Thus each week a new chairman of all business meetings is appointed. (Here is the building or re-building of "community" so like the rest of the work of All Saints' – so like, we would think, Jesus of Nazareth, who, after healing a man, was anxious for his return to the community.)

(2) Gradually to break up the patient's dependence on the hospital and other "total institutions", to avoid the well-known "institutional syndrome", to help the patient build up his strength and rely more on the health and social services of his own community. Thus the Centre acts as a bridge between the hospital and the community-at-large, a "take-off platform" from which patients can test their preparedness to reach out into the community as fully responsible members.

(3) To re-integrate – or integrate for the first time – the group member into his own community. Here help is given to clients in finding a room in which to live, in obtaining a part-time job, in filling up application forms for Ontario Housing, in interviewing O.H.C. officials. A relationship is also formed with local community-workers, health-resource people, and agencies in the community. Outings and excursions are made to organizations and places of interest in the area and city.

(4) To be responsive to the different needs and many problems of people in the community, and to

establish a giving and receiving spirit with other local services, with the ultimate aim of realizing a complete community health service in the area.

As the report states:

> In these ways the Centre is helping people to re-enter, to feel more connected to, their own community – by helping them to become more aware of the various health and social services, and cultural activities around them, then in supporting them in their efforts to use them . . . .

While I cannot, of course, relate case-histories, it is good to hear personal experiences of help received at the Dundas Day-Care Centre. Here are the words of one client: "I am much happier since I left the hospital. I think it is a great opportunity to meet in a church and forget the unpleasant experience of hospitalization." Another client has found that here "people really care about me and my problems . . . It has helped me to see so many people improving in their outlook . . . A place such as this one has long been needed." Also, a letter was published in the *Ward 7 News* (May 21, 1970) from a former patient whom it was my pleasure to know well. He wrote:

> I personally know that the Dundas Day Centre, located at the Church at the corner of Sherbourne and Dundas, has been and is now a success in the community. This Day Centre has been helping many patients to return to their community as healthier people and to stay out of mental hospitals, where they have been institutionalized for ten years or longer.

Throughout, we have enjoyed happy relations with the staff and clients of this clinic. The nurses have been all that nurses should or can be, and Elsie, their leader, is absolutely first-class and completely dedicated. A doctor is always most ready to help. The clinic staff have helped us out in emergencies in the Friendship Centre, in our reception room, and at the Open Door, which was first staffed by former clients of the Dundas Day-Care Centre.

After nearly two years, the Centre was obliged to move away from our buildings, but we still have a hot-line to them. On a recent occasion, two nurses went in to see a very elderly sick man who would not allow us to call a doctor; the nurses were able to visit him in the guise of social workers. On another occasion, a frighteningly large Maritimer came in to see us in a very emotional state; how wonderful then to have experts all round us. I got almost nowhere with him; Ed, our caretaker, got only a bit further. But Elsie was so patient with him, so loving, that it put us professional Christians to shame; she found he was a veteran and got him to Sunnybrook Hospital. We shared happy times too with the patients – an occasional dance, or our Men's Club bingo afternoons, and they, as well as the nurses, still drop in to see us, come to the Open Door or the Agape Supper.

For quite a time after the Centre had officially left us, a Work Programme operated in the gym. This involved a project of rehabilitating old clothing, and at the same time ourselves; the clothing was sold in a community clothing store. Now we have this little store in a corner of the church – chiefly, we repeat, as a rehabilitation exercise for a patient or two. Also there was a small "sheltered workshop" which met with about twelve men in the gym, but it has moved for the sake of space into the side aisle of the church.

We are happy to hear from a nurse that the re-admission rate to the Centre is quite low, and that the general idea of meeting people outside the hospital seems to have earned approval and become well-accepted. It was, after all, almost a pilot-project. We have been told by doctors and nurses that the church has helped in this "outreach", this missionary movement, and we feel happy that the Church of Christ has in some little way at All Saints' assisted in continuing the work of Jesus in healing them that are bruised, in "casting out demons from those that are possessed".

CHAPTER XIV
OUT OF CHRISTIAN CONCERN

It has been our object to gather in and around our buildings as many services and agencies as possible to assist the people of our neighbourhood. The people here have so little resources or talent to live a normal life with their families in a world that can be pretty tough. As we looked around after becoming acquainted with the place, it didn't take long to sum up the most vital needs of the people in the community. These involved poverty, sickness of body and mind, alcoholism and in some cases drug addiction, poor homes or none, unemployment, loneliness, incapacity of age or disability, the strangeness of life for the migrant or immigrant, as well as breakdown of marriage and family life. And in nearly all of these needs we have, with the help of some very good people, made an attempt to assist. We have done this primarily because we want to help people; it is the natural response of being Christian and loving people. Also we hope that in all this we are doing and showing the gospel. If in helping a person's material needs we also bring him into a love-relationship with Christ and his fellowmen, we believe that we have given an extra, immeasurable gift. But we do not try to meet people merely in order to get another body in the pew!

The larger of these service groups, such as the Friendship Centre, the Open Door and the Room Registry, the Indian services, and the Mental Health Centre, have already been described. However, we would like briefly to mention others. Some of them have come to us; others we have invited to come. Of course, we have a glorious opportunity presented to the church at this moment, in the many L.I.P. grants and projects, as well as those under the Opportunities for Youth (O.F.Y.). All of these people are looking for space, and that is something we have.

Legal-Aid Counselling

An old member of the church once wrote to me of the wonderful history of All Saints', and how all the judges and lawyers used to live in our parish. I wanted to reply to her that we hadn't any judges living there now, but that plenty of people from the neighbourhood are greatly occupied with the law.

It very soon became apparent to us that many people here needed legal advice, mostly about fairly small problems, though these are of course of great concern to those who have them. It may be difficult for them to get quick attention and many are hesitant to go to law offices. So we asked the University Law School if they would like to send a legal "missionary" to our area. And at just about that time the Law School members were thinking of the same thing; perhaps they also had been watching the TV show about the "Storefront Lawyers". Our request was favourably received, and we were visited by a deputation from the University Law School who looked about the place and were impressed with the number of bodies around. They told us they had been operating in the area of the University Settlement, and that they would like to move in to us. I think we were about the second such place to have this free legal aid counselling service; I believe now there are about twenty-five clinics, mostly downtown.

Law students visit such places as the Neighbourhood Information Post, the Indian Centre on Beverley Street, Dixon Hall and some churches and community centres, among them All Saints' for an afternoon and an evening each week. I want to testify to the interest and zeal of these students, their care in following up cases, their patience with some of the people, their readiness to protect them. These men and women seem quite dedicated to alleviating the lot of the poor and under-privileged and inarticulate. I find this a healthy sign for the future of society.

Of course, their work is limited by the fact that they are not full lawyers, but they are able to deal with lesser criminal cases and can go to court with clients in matters involving claims under $400. They assist in such things as filling up income tax forms (a necessary service to any but the highly intelligent), making out simple wills, and helping with immigration and landlord-tenant problems. They deal a lot with agencies such as Welfare and Unemployment Assistance; so often it happens that for some reason or another the monthly cheque does not come. The students are also able to advise in matters of marriage and divorce. In an area of quite considerable domestic confusion, and of little education, there are so many of these problems. Their main service is to advise people how to proceed, and to direct them, if advisable, to the legal aid authorities; but sometimes they merely listen to grievances, and give people cónfidence. They perform a very worthwhile service to the community; they fill a few of the needs of the people, and we are very happy to have them with us.

Alcoholics Anonymous

We sought the help of the A.A. for a couple of years, assured that we could offer them a really happy hunting-ground. Now they meet here every Monday – any Monday, whether it be Christmas Day or Thanksgiving, for the enemy never takes a rest. The main difficulty in my parish is that people may come in too intoxicated to know what is going on; for example, we never knew that George used to drink till one day he came in sober.

It is a difficult place, where alcoholism is the way of life, where not too many "drunks" really want to give up if they could. Perhaps it is only the eagerly expected cheque, and the anticipated binge, that adds anything at all to the lives of some of these chaps. Alcohol is the curse of this district; whatever problem afflicts the family, it is caused, or intensified, or affected in one way or another by excessive drinking. Through this I see my good friends making asses of themselves, making themselves a ruddy nuisance to everyone. I can see them today as I write, coming for food for "their starving children", while reeking so strongly with the stuff that I would be afraid to light a match. At other times they will be weeping in self-pity, or clinging to you like a child to his mother's apron-strings. I see men whom I know, whom I have come to think of with affection, drinking themselves to death, deteriorating every year, becoming older-looking, greyer, their brains weaker, till – like one man I saw in hospital with his skin bright yellow, almost a livid orange colour, due to some liver complaint – they meet a solitary death and equally solitary funeral, with perhaps no mourner save the parson. For so few really want to stop drinking . . . *But some few do want to stop, and with God's grace they succeed.* They become sober and continue in sobriety, and thank God for the A.A. and the wonderful people who lead it.

David started the group in our church. He had been given up as a hopeless alcoholic. He took his first drink at the age of nine, and says he hardly stopped since. At twelve years he couldn't make up his mind whether to be the biggest or the best drunk in town. He was an expert at mixing rubbing alcohol with various potations, though he admits that he never in all his varied experience actually consumed shoe polish. He suffered much from DT's and during those times he saw things moving about. Not only did he see snakes, but he tried to hit them with a frying-pan. Rats vividly chased up the front of his legs; when he got them from there, they would run up the back of his legs. At such moments he would fling himself against the wall to shake them off, so real would they be. So he touched bottom, and really wanted to become sober. This sincere desire to be sober is what so many people really lack. He took his last drink of a quart of whiskey, and then stopped. He attributes his success to his taking the third step in the A.A. programme: "The decision to turn our will and our life over to the care of God, as we understand Him, and every night to thank our Higher Power for keeping us sober that day." For a time he would keep up a twenty-minute sobriety action – keep sober for one twenty-minute stretch at a time, and then the next twenty. He now adds to his nightly prayer of thanks for keeping sober that day, the petition "In what way can I help God tomorrow?"

Children's Groups

We have, of course, always had a number of the usual church activities for children. A wonderful story could be told of how, in the past, 1,000 children came to our Sunday school. Recently we have had the usual groups such as Cubs and Scouts (a very strong group with many trophies), Youth Group, Servers and Junior Chancel Guild. We have managed to carry on most of these with reasonable success, though often frustrating and disappointing, and often short of leadership or support for the leaders when we have them. This is not an area where many children live or where large families can find accomodation; for these we have to go to Regent Park. There is also the difficult fact that nearly all the children whom we meet come from broken homes, and many regrettably will follow in the same tradition. Quite a number have learning disabilities or are emotionally disturbed. Most do not possess, and do not seem to be encouraged to acquire, the self-discipline which will let them rise out of the welfare bracket. And probably most of the children do not get enough sleep or the right kind of food.

There have been some specific children's activities

of a regular type organized within our buildings and looked after by various groups and projects. The school meals (a daily breakfast and lunch) for the Duke of York School were managed and served in our building a few years ago. We are daily waiting for a similar project of school breakfast and dinner for about fifty children, with After-School Care and summer activities, to open in our Baldwin Hall. This will be managed by one of our church leaders in connection with Lord Dufferin School. Some children will pay and others will be supported. We hope that this will help especially where parents are either very poor and do not understand about basic nutrition, or where parents are at work.

During the early winter and the summer of 1973, children's programmes were run daily under grants from L.I.P. and the Opportunities for Youth programme. The first was for little children and their mothers, but it was difficult to get mothers to want to do anything other than dump their children in a nursery and then get lost. When this programme developed into a day nursery without the benefit of mothers, numbers grew, however. There were children's films, a very fine toy library, and summer and camping outings.

Not unrelated with this activity for children and families was a community dress-making group who gave instruction in sewing and dress-making. Then there was the previously mentioned rehabilitation group from the Dundas Day Care Mental Health Centre – women repairing clothes which they sold at a nearby store, while a group of former male patients had a kind of small "sheltered workshop". All these activities gave the Baldwin Hall a very happy and lively spirit; it almost developed into a small community centre of its own. A mid-day meal was served and quite a number of workers as well as the children and visitors would come in and share their lunch in a very "homey" atmosphere.

Dental Care

The newest health project is a free – or nearly free – dental clinic. Plans are going ahead for this slowly, but apparently surely; it is a matter of finding the funding. (I am told that some of the services will pay for teeth to be taken out, but will not put them in again.) The need for this is very great; apparently there is only one dentist in the neighbourhood, and it is very hard to get an appointment. Through the activities of S.O.C.C.A. (South of Carlton Community Action) and assisted by the D.C.A. (Downtown Church-Workers Association), we expect that this clinic will be operating soon. The community approached us about using our buildings; we told them we would welcome the dentist with open arms and with open mouths. How often I have heard people say they would rather get a tooth out than come to church; here is a unique opportunity to do both at the same time. Even the sermon will help: it can be piped in over an intercom, thereby saving anaesthetic, and we guarantee that the patient will sleep peacefully during anything which the dentist can do to our mortal bodies.

'Come-Together' Club

This club has recently been started by a nurse working at Queen Street Mental Health Hospital. It meets weekly for an evening of entertainment and friendship for people who are *lonely*. Many of us believe that acute loneliness is one of the causes of breakdown and much unhappiness. This club attempts to bring lonely single people together. As quite a few comers are former patients from Queen Street or the Dundas Day Care Centre, we are very happy for this further connection with the work of mental health, and with the staff and personnel of Dundas Day Care Centre.

Employment Services

There have been several employment agencies working with grants from L.I.P. Many of these ask a percentage of income from each man for whom they find a job. However, because of its L.I.P. funding, a group called CRUNCH was able to give such services free. This group was with us for a summer, finding mostly casual jobs. I met them first when I was talking to a man who had just come from the penitentiary; he needed home and work. The man from CRUNCH walked in and was immediately able to offer him both. Employment – one of the most pressing needs of the people of our community: it was good to have this agency with us for a short time at least.

Overnight Drop-In Centre

This has been our most recent field of endeavour. I had often said that the place should be open all night, and manned by a staff of competent people. I realized this in all its stark fury one midnight after the New Year's Watch-Night service, when the whole area seemed to break loose and go wild, resembling Virgil's account of the sacking of Troy, though it would be hard to say on which side the local inhabitants might be.

We were therefore interested when we received a deputation from the local community group, led by Elsie Norton, chairman of S.O.C.C.A., applying for space to run an Overnight Drop-In Centre. They had operated for almost a year in the Central Neighbourhood House, but now their lease was terminated. As Elsie Norton wrote in a letter of September 11, 1973:

> The Overnight Drop-In has always existed to *serve the people in the community*; to serve people who are lonely, poor or burdened with many human problems. I personally know that for many people the Drop-In has been a place – perhaps the only place in the city – where they have felt genuinely welcomed and accepted, and have received whatever help and warmth they needed to get back on their feet again, or simply to feel more alive and human.
>
> The Drop-In, I believe, has been a powerful source of hope for many people; it has performed a truly Christian act, in the most basic sense of the term. If being Christian means anything, I believe it means sharing with people, spiritual rebirth, providing a haven for the lonely and oppressed, hope. This is what the Overnight Drop-In is about.

After several meetings we decided to take the risk – a risk because we knew that in the middle of the night we would meet a great variety of characters, and no doubt at some time or other run into some serious problem, crisis, crime, or violence that might be committed on our premises. We opened some weeks before Christmas, and, as far as I am aware, with success and satisfaction. The Centre is presently open in the Baldwin Hall three nights a week, Friday, Saturday, and Sunday, from eleven p.m. to eight a.m. Sandwiches and coffee are provided inexpensively. People play cards in one room, watch TV in another, or go to sleep. We try to resist its becoming a free "flop-house" or "doss-house", for we are not in competition with the local rooming-houses. However, some do come here who have no place to sleep or are too late to check in at the local hostels, or too inebriated to be acceptable. Others come because they are lonely and cannot sleep, or are tired of their one room, and can't stand the sight of their own four walls. Some come in crisis; some are referred to this place where they may stay the night. Some are brought in by the police. Some have just come to the city and don't know where to go. Occasionally someone who is not down-and-out comes in; this was the case with a lawyer who once demanded to stay and made a donation of $100.

We once had a very good documentary about the "Overnight" on the C.B.C. "Weekday" programme following the evening news. This contained interviews with the leader and other workers and guests, including myself. Pictures of the church were also shown, and it was introduced as a church in Cabbagetown that was relevant to the situation and whose leaders had courage. It was concluded by words from the anchorman, Bill Lawrence: "It seems to me that this is Christianity."

CHAPTER XV
THE FUTURE OF ALL SAINTS'

What of the future? Where do we go from here? From a desert there has been created a thriving city; from a wilderness a place where many people come. Almost a little empire has been built; will it decline and fall, or does it go forward to greater and new advances? For there is, after all, the rejuvenating force that the Romans lacked – the moving, ever-youthful Spirit of God.

Circumstances beyond our control will decide and dictate future policy. The whole area of our parish is in process of reconstruction and of planning for reconstruction. A vivid instance is provided by the building immediately to the south of us, right by the church wall – two high-rise towers of semi-luxury type apartments, for well-to-do, middle-income people. To the north of us, the old houses on Sherbourne Street are to be restored, if they don't fall down first, and town-houses will be built behind them. Right across from the church on Dundas Street, stores and apartments will be built. Some of these will be occupied by poor people, but others by the middle-income group. In the area of Moss Park another large building of Ontario Housing is being occupied. Whenever a new house is built on a vacant lot or replaces an old one, the cost is perhaps $50,000 – beyond the reach of poor people. Also, middle-class people – especially "arty" or historic types – are buying up some of the ugly late Victorian houses which fill their artistic souls with romance.

It looks very much as though the poor people will by degrees be driven out of the area – where to, God only knows, and the opposition can only tell. Families with children are tending to move away to Ontario Housing in the suburbs, as they probably should do. It is doubtful that the smoke of the city and the atmosphere of skid row and the general drunkenness are the right setting in which to raise a family... But skid row may itself move away; it will be continually harder for single men to find the horrible cheap rooming-houses where they have existed for years. If I may offer any forecast for the neighbourhood, it will probably become one of mixed income, with middle-class people living in high-rise apartments completely oblivious to the community around them on the ground. There will also be a considerable amount of Ontario Housing for poorer people, and an element of skid row as long as the missions stay in the district.

The tendency of middle-class people to live down in the old slums is a strange turn of events for All Saints', as it is unusual for the whole of North America. It is almost ironic that the moment we got our place geared for a mission in skid row, immediately at that time and immediately next door to us, a middle-class set-up began to emerge. For years All Saints' *had* worked hard to run a middle-class church in a slum area: eventually, as we have described, we were able to pull out of the middle-class culture, and create a church where poor people might feel at home. And just when we have done this, there is an influx of middle-income people. We have ourselves become used to seeing characters sitting on the doorsteps of the church; we have become accustomed to climbing over the bodies of inebriated parishioners to get into the building. But will the new middle-class parishioners in their mink coats be so happy about this? Or will they regard us with the same hostility that the people in Moss Park feel towards the Salvation Army Hostel right by their doors? Will the new middle-class people adapt to the kind of ministry we are presently offering?

Adaptability – this must be the password, the password to life, survival, immortality! This was the word that Bishop Snell emphasized to us at our Centennial, speaking of the way we had tried to adapt to the changing conditions. We will have to adapt very readily to new situations if they arise, and maybe we will have to adapt back again. It will probably be a long while before the poor and needy leave the district altogether; perhaps they never will. But it is possible that skid row may move across the Don River; who really knows? Then, if All Saints' is true to her principles of serving the people around her, and if those people become middle-class, then we must sacrifice our inverted snobbery and assume a middle-class ministry once again – a bit hard, but obviously our duty because middle-class people have souls too!

If this should happen, if the surrounding population should be employed through the day, then our present daily ministry may be no longer necessary. A more compact building may suffice, when we are no longer in the centre of an idle population. Perhaps we should think of our future as built in the heart of a large high-rise complex offering all sorts of services, as well as housing, with the church as the nerve-centre – the place of feeling in the structure of a very large building. Or we may be in between a number of high-rise complexes, or perhaps in little churches within a number of buildings. For, according to the principle we established earlier, the church must serve the people of the parish, whether they are millionaires or down-and-outs. Of course, some of us may opt out and move with our friends of skid row across the Don River or wherever they go; it may be our personal duty to assist the ministry there. But the work of All Saints' would still be where she stands and serves.

We sincerely trust that the economic factor will not be the deciding one. It is a matter of difficulty to finance a church downtown, especially if the congregation is very poor. We probably give away through the week to poor people as much as we take in at the Sunday collection. I am quite aware of this – but if we want poor people to come to church, it will probably have to be a church of poor people only. We have seen in our case that if the older congregation remains a middle-class type, then the whole tone of the place will be middle-class; they pay the piper and so they call the tune. But the poor and the inarticulate should begin to have a share in the planning of their church. It should be their own church, an indigenous church. This means it will be related to the feelings of Cabbagetown (if it is in Cabbagetown) and not an outpost of Etobicoke and of Etobicokism down in the inner city.

If this is so, then the "successful" clergyman in a poor parish will be one who has a congregation of poor people. But, at the same time, if he has such a congregation, he will be unsuccessful in that the collections will be tiny; the church will not be able to pay its way, will be thrown out of Synod, and the minister will be catalogued as a failure because he is not sending money out to Borrioboola-Gha. So it is almost impossible to do a good job in the slums and keep one's church open. The Sunday collection may only be about $35 from fifty people, because the welfare cheque doesn't allow for church collections. Quite obviously such churches must be regarded as mission churches and support-ed as such, just as are the missions in the hinter-land of Ontario or in darkest Africa.

For we must realize this: a missionary inner-city church does not cater to a regular clientele of es-tablished worshippers who belong there forever. It serves, rather, people who have dropped out of every parish in the diocese, as well as every diocese in Canada and new immigrants from overseas. Nor is it kept open for the faithful few on Sunday, but for the masses from all over the country, who for mostly sad reasons have come to live down here –

the bad boy who went wrong in Oshawa, the old chorister who left home in Manitoba, the town drunk from Peterborough, the failure from Forest Hill, the girl from England who had a nervous breakdown, the occasional West Indian who didn't make it over here. These are imaginary people, but they are also very real; these are our people. The church on Toronto's skid row serves people of every parish in the diocese, and of the whole Canadian Church, and therefore should be supported by the church at large – and must be if we are to continue to care for the drop-outs of all our society.

An equally good case could be made for the claim that, because most of what we do does not strictly come under the category of religion but, if you like, social service, we have a right to be financially supported by the state. In no sense are we denominational here; we don't ask a man if he is an Anglican before we give him a cup of coffee, or before we start to pull out his teeth at the Dental Clinic. We would therefore reasonably hope that funds from the city or province or nation would assist us as we give up our buildings to keep people off the street by day and night, with all the attendent expense involved. In fact, so far we have been able to find more support from the government and from secular organizations than we have from the Church, although new hope is coming from this latter direction. We are, after all, something of an experiment, and I suppose we must prove ourselves. I realize, too, that other needs come before the authorities as well as ours, and that in a world of starvation, many of these needs are more pressing.

So the future is quite uncertain. Probably for some years there will be no shattering change in the direction of our ministry, though we already notice a few odd people walking around in their own tailor-made clothes, smoking their own tailor-made cigarettes. We may even have one or two cars on the parking-lot on a Sunday. But because the *distant* future is uncertain, it is therefore exciting. As long as we are ready to adapt, and also do not worry about who gets the credit for what we do, then we feel assured that we at All Saints' will have lots of fun.

APPENDIX: A SUGGESTED FORM OF SERVICE FOR THE LORD'S SUPPER

We offer a form of service based on the works of Gregory Dix,[1] Charles Moule,[2] John Kirby,[3] and others. This is meant to resemble what we imagine would be the pattern of the Eucharist of the Primitive Church, and much of it is culled from the accounts of early Christian worship in the writings of the early Fathers.

There might be a table for the President and his assistants to officiate, and other tables set in the form of a circle or horseshoe. There might also be an additional table to receive gifts for the poor.

(1) When all are seated – for it was the Jewish custom to sit to partake of the bread, and to stand for the receiving of the cup[4] – the President will

---

[1] Dom. Gregory Dix, *The Shape of the Liturgy* (London: Westminster, 1945).

[2] C. F. D. Moule, *Worship in the New Testament* (London: Lutterworth Press, 1961), p. 33 ff.

[3] John Kirby, *The Kingdom, the Power and the Glory* (Toronto: The Anglican Church of Canada, 1963), p. 116 ff.

[4] Dom. Gregory Dix, *The Shape of the Liturgy*, p. 8.

begin with the Blessing over the Bread, a prayer which may be long or short. The *Didache* recommends the use of a fixed form;[5] we offer as a sample something of the following:

PRESIDENT: The Lord be with you.

ALL: And with they spirit.

PRESIDENT: Lift up your hearts.

ALL: We lift them all up unto the Lord.

PRESIDENT: Let us give thanks unto the Lord *(this was the invitation of the president in the chaburah meal for all to participate in the prayer)*.

ALL: It is right that we do so.

PRESIDENT: It is very right that we give thanks to Thee, O Lord, for all Thy goodness and loving-kindness to us and to all men. We bless Thee for our creation, preservation, and all the blessings of this life, but above all for Thine inestimable love in the redemption of the world by our Lord Jesus Christ. (*Here a Proper for the season may be added*). We give thanks (*eucharistoumen*) unto Thee, our Father, for the life and knowledge which Thou didst make known to us through Jesus Christ Thy servant. Glory be to Thee for ever ... As this bread that is broken was scattered upon the mountains and gathered together and became one, so let Thy Church be gathered together from the ends of the earth into Thy Kingdom, for Thine is the glory and the power, through Jesus for ever.[6] The night on which He was betrayed, that very night, our Lord took bread, gave thanks and broke it, say-

---

[5] *Didache*: 10:7. (Written in about A.D. 110, this gives a description of the Eucharist and Agape.)

[6] Ibid., 9:4.

ing, "Take and eat: This is my body which is given for you." So may the body of our Lord Jesus Christ preserve Thy body and soul unto eternal life.

During these words the President will break the bread and care will be taken for the distribution to all present. Other eulogia (which are really meant to be blessings of God for the gift of bread, rather than blessings of the bread itself, as would first appear in our "graces") might be taken from such writings as Ephesians 1 and I Peter 1.

(2) The Supper will then proceed, the Agape. Here would be normal, happy conversation of people renewing old acquaintances and making new ones . . . natural fellowship.

(3) When supper is over, then there will follow the Blessing or Thanksgiving over the cup:

PRESIDENT: *(all standing)* The Lord be with you.

ALL: And with thy spirit.

PRESIDENT: Are you able to drink of the cup that I drink, and be baptized with the baptism that I am baptized with? *(Here follows a moment for serious reflection.)* We thank Thee, our Father, for the holy wine of David Thy servant, which Thou didst make known to us through Jesus Christ Thy servant, Glory be to Thee forever.[7] To His ancient people of Israel God gave deliverance from bondage in Egypt, and brought them to a land flowing with milk and honey, in accord with the covenant which He gave. Now hear the new covenant which our Lord gives to us who once were not a people, but are now the

---

[7] Ibid., 9:2.

People of God, the new Israel . . . It was after supper, that night on which He was betrayed, that our Lord took the cup, and gave thanks, and gave it to His disciples saying: "This is the cup of the new covenant in my blood, my life which I give for you for the remission of your sins. Remember me as often as you drink this cup." *(Here the president will sip the cup, and all others, either from the same or from separate cups. Then all stand.)* And in his cup we pledge ourselves his soldiers and servants unto our lives' ends, and may the cup of the new covenant preserve thy body and soul unto eternal life.

ALL: Here, O Lord, we offer ourselves, our souls and bodies, a sacrifice unto Thee.

The worship may end with a suitable benediction, preferably "Go forth into the world in peace . . . ", and the singing of a Psalm or hymn, according to the custom of the chaburah meal.[8]

(4) In addition to this, and to accompany it, depending on the place, number of people, occasion, hymns such as "Fairest Lord Jesus" or "Hail Gladdening Light" might be sung. (A nice touch is added in an eastern rite, which has found its way into the *Apostolic Tradition*: "Having risen after supper, the children and virgins shall sing praises by the light of the lamp".[9]) There would also be readings from the Old and New Testaments if desired, or from similarly inspired writings. A talk might be given, or a play or act of drama, or

---

[8] Dom. Gregory Dix, *The Shape of the Liturgy*, p. 58. Also, Mark 14:26.

[9] Hippolytus, *The Apostolic Tradition*, xxvi.

music. There might also be discussion together or in groups, with the provision that the more inarticulate be given a chance to speak and be encouraged to express their feelings.

(5) At the early "Breaking of Bread" there was a strong emphasis on charity; the very agape-meal itself was a blessing to the poor and needy families. We suggest that the last part of any Christian Agape or Eucharist be a care of the needy — "concern", almost in the manner of allocating jobs at a service club. Thus jobs may be allocated to each member – the care of the sick and needy, the visiting of homes and hospitals, the care of the lonely and disturbed people, the staffing of social and welfare organizations and children's activities. This is an adaptation of the ancient act of worship into a simple form for today, especially for rather simple and not necessarily church-oriented people.

BIBLIOGRAPHY

Boyd, Malcolm, *The Underground Church*. New York: Sheed & Ward, 1968.

Dix, Dom. Gregory, *The Shape of the Liturgy*. London: Westminster, 1945.

Jungman, J. A., *The Early Liturgy to the Time of Gregory the Great*. Translated by Francis A. Brunner. Notre Dame, Ind.: University of Notre Dame Press, 1959.

Kirby, John C., *The Kingdom, the Power and the Glory*. Toronto: The Anglican Church of Canada, 1963.

Moule, Charles F. D., *Worship in the New Testament*. London: Lutterworth Press, 1961.

Oesterley, O.E., *The Jewish Background of the Sacraments*. Dacre Press, 1945.

Robinson, John A. T., *On Being the Church in the World: Essays*. London: S.C.M. Press, 1960.

—*The New Reformation*. London, S.C.M. Press, 1965.

For early celebrations of the Agape see also:

Cyprian. *Epistles;* lxiii: 16

Hippolytus. *The Apostolic Tradition:* xxvi: 18-32.

Tertullian. *Apologeticus*, 39.

PaperJacks

PaperJacks, the newest addition to General Publishing Co. Ltd. (one of the few Canadian book companies owned by Canadians), is the most exciting and innovative Canadian mass market paperback programme in Canada. Designed to introduce for the first time in paperback both Canadian books formerly published in hard cover and original works by Canadian authors, PaperJacks includes in its list such noted writers as Robert Thomas Allen, Tom Ardies, Margaret Atwood, Claude Aubry, John B. Ballem, Jack Batten, Clark Blaise, Harry Boyle, Sheila Burnford, Eugène Cloutier, Raymond de Coccola & Paul King, David Conover, Kildare Dobbs, Marian Engel, Alan Fry, Mavis Gallant, Anne Hébert, Piet Hein, Harold Horwood, E. Pauline Johnson, Donald Johnston, Drs. Harold & Oriana Josseau Kalant, Ronald A. Keith, Thomas P. Kelley, Helen Marquis, Fredelle Bruser Maynard, Brian Moore, Audrey Y. Morris, Eric Nicol, Mordecai Richler, R. D. Symons, and Delbert A. Young.

In a short time, PaperJacks has set industry-wide precedents, and will continue to provide good mass market books by important Canadian authors – books which are needed by Canadians at prices they can afford.

PaperJacks

TO UNDERSTAND JEWS
by Stuart E. Rosenberg

Superbly enlightening, this book clarifies Jewish views on immortality, sex, sin, marriage, the "closeness" of the Jewish people, the Messiah and other significant points. It describes the evolution of Jewish culture and religion from biblical times to the present. Simple eloquence and lucidity rip through the veils of ignorance and misunderstanding to open the way towards one of man's noblest goals: the recognition of human brotherhood. $1.25

THE SACRED MUSHROOM AND THE CROSS
by John M. Allegro

After a thorough study of the etymology of the Sumerian and Middle Eastern Languages, *John Allegro* has formed a startling theory about the origin of Christianity. He has traced the existence of a mushroom cult which, because of its drug-taking practices, was cloaked in a respectable myth about an historical Jesus. This is fascinating and thought-provoking reading. $1.50

PaperJacks

THE PURSUIT OF INTOXICATION
by Andrew I. Malcolm, M.D.

The effects of such controversial drugs as marijuana, LSD, mescaline and speed are discussed by Dr. Andrew Malcolm, a Toronto psychiatrist, who was formerly with the Ontario Addiction Research Foundation. He examines the use of psychoactive substances in many societies throughout history and considers their application under five broad categories: Religion, Medicine, Endurance, Extinction and Recreation. $1.25

DRUGS, SOCIETY AND PERSONAL CHOICE
by Harold Kalant and Oriana Josseau Kalant

In recent years, there has been a great public demand for knowledge about drugs. However, the conflicting information which has inundated Canadians has only added to the confusion. *Drugs, Society and Personal Choice* provides data which will enable responsible citizens to form a perspective in order to intelligently evaluate the evidence and form their own balanced decisions about government policy. $1.95

PaperJacks

MEMORIES OF A CATHOLIC BOYHOOD
by Harry Boyle

In this highly personal account, popular Canadian author Harry Boyle writes about the pangs and pleasures of his adolescence in rural Ontario during the Depression. Urged by his mother toward the priesthood, the author attended St. Gerald's, a low-cost, all-male Catholic college and it was here that he changed from a country boy to a budding author – and life within its strict walls is recalled with fondness and hilarity. $1.50

GENTLE PIONEERS
Five Nineteenth-Century Canadians
by Audrey Y. Morris

To the harsh pioneering land of Upper Canada in the 1830s came Susanna Moodie, John W. Dunbar Moodie, Catharine Parr Traill, Thomas Traill and Samuel Strickland. This brilliant biography of a family group shows these people not just as literary and historical personages, but as the individuals they were, with human weaknesses and frailties. It is a vivid portrait of a group who lived through appalling hardships to become noble and "gentle pioneers". $1.50

PaperJacks

AYORAMA

by Raymond de Coccola and Paul King

This is the poignant, often shocking story of
the Krangmalit – "The People Beyond" – a
primitive people who live in the Canadian
Central Arctic. Their story is heroic, from
the opening scene of birth in an isolated
igloo to the final disaster wrought by an
epidemic that rages through a whole
encampment. Raymond de Coccola spent
twelve years as an Oblate missionary among
the Krangmalit, and, assisted by Paul King,
he describes vividly their unwritten laws, cus-
toms, and character – the unvarnished truth
of man's behaviour at the furthest limits of
human endurance. $1.95

WITHOUT RESERVE

by Sheila Burnford
with drawings by Susan Ross

Two women fulfill a dream – to visit the
remote reserves of the Cree and Ojibwa
Indians. *Without Reserve* is a moving reflection of the life of these vulnerable people as
captured in the writing of Sheila Burnford,
author of the bestselling *The Incredible Journey*, and the drawings of her friend, artist
Susan Ross. $1.75

PaperJacks

WHITE ESKIMO
by Harold Horwood

For some men, Esau Gillingham was the authentic hero, the "White Spirit" of Eskimo legends. For others, particularly the White Establishment, he was a corrupter of the innocent, a renegade, and finally a murderer. The dramatic account of three cultures – White, Indian, and Eskimo – colliding in the Arctic wilderness. $1.50

HOW A PEOPLE DIE
by Alan Fry

This documentary novel offers a searingly honest look at life among Canadian Indians today. Drawing on his experience as an Indian agent in Western Canada, Alan Fry vividly portrays the squalor and despair of most Indians' daily lives, and examines the agonizing dilemmas that confront the white men who seek to help them.

The novel focuses on a single event, the shocking death of an infant Indian girl through the apparent neglect of her parents. But it reflects a broader, more disturbing question: How can a people live in a world almost totally alien to them? $1.50

PaperJacks

THE LAW AND THE POLICE
by John Eisenberg and Paula Bourne

When individual rights are infringed in the course of law enforcement, controversy inevitably arises. Recent examples of this are explored here, involving the use of force by police, the invasion of the privacy of suspected criminals, and the granting of special powers to the police by the War Measures Act. *$1.25*

DON'T TEACH THAT!
by John Eisenberg and Gailand MacQueen

Who has the right to teach matters of personal belief? Governments often introduce programs for teaching sex, religion, politics, and morals in the schools. Parents protest, claiming it is their responsibility within the family. Read this probing inquiry into a widely debated question. *$1.25*